# Amália at the Olympia

# 33 1/3 Global

**33 1/3 Global**, a series related to but independent from **33 1/3**, takes the format of the original series of short, music-based books and brings the focus to music throughout the world. With initial volumes focusing on Japanese and Brazilian music, the series will also include volumes on the popular music of Australia/Oceania, Europe, Africa, the Middle East, and more.

## 33 1/3 Japan

Series Editor: Noriko Manabe

Spanning a range of artists and genres—from the 1970s rock of Happy End to technopop band Yellow Magic Orchestra, the Shibuya-kei of Cornelius, classic anime series *Cowboy Bebop,* J-Pop/EDM hybrid Perfume, and vocaloid star Hatsune Miku—**33 1/3 Japan** is a series devoted to in-depth examination of Japanese popular music of the twentieth and twenty-first centuries.

Published Titles:

Supercell's *Supercell* by Keisuke Yamada

*AKB48* by Patrick W. Galbraith and Jason G. Karlin

Yoko Kanno's *Cowboy Bebop Soundtrack* by Rose Bridges

Perfume's *Game* by Patrick St. Michel

Cornelius's *Fantasma* by Martin Roberts

Joe Hisaishi's *My Neighbor Totoro: Soundtrack* by Kunio Hara

Shonen Knife's *Happy Hour* by Brooke McCorkle

Nenes' *Koza Dabasa* by Henry Johnson

Yuming's *The 14th Moon* by Lasse Lehtonen

Forthcoming Titles:

Yellow Magic Orchestra's *Yellow Magic Orchestra* by Toshiyuki Ohwada

Kohaku utagassen: The Red and White Song Contest by Shelley Brunt

# Amália at the Olympia

Lila Ellen Gray

Series Editor: Fabian Holt

BLOOMSBURY ACADEMIC
NEW YORK • LONDON • OXFORD • NEW DELHI • SYDNEY

BLOOMSBURY ACADEMIC
Bloomsbury Publishing Inc
1385 Broadway, New York, NY 10018, USA
50 Bedford Square, London, WC1B 3DP, UK
29 Earlsfort Terrace, Dublin 2, Ireland

BLOOMSBURY, BLOOMSBURY ACADEMIC and the Diana logo are
trademarks of Bloomsbury Publishing Plc

First published in the United States of America 2023

Library of Congress Cataloging-in-Publication Data

Names: Gray, Lila Ellen, 1966, author.
Title: Amália at the Olympia / Lila Ellen Gray.
Description: [1st.] | New York : Bloomsbury Academic, 2023. | Series: 33
1/3 Europe | Includes bibliographical references and index. | Summary:
"Examines Amália Rodrigues's seminal international hit album, recorded
live at the Paris Olympia in 1956"-- Provided by publisher.
Identifiers: LCCN 2022058944 (print) | LCCN 2022058945 (ebook) | ISBN
9781501346200 (hardback) | ISBN 9781501346194 (paperback) | ISBN
9781501346217 (ebook) | ISBN 9781501346224 (pdf) | ISBN
9781501346231 (ebook other)
Subjects: LCSH: Rodrigues, Amália, 1920–1999. Amalia à l'Olympia. |
Fados--History and criticism.
Classification: LCC ML420.R755 G73 2023  (print) | LCC ML420.R755
(ebook) | DDC 782.42162/691092--dc23/eng/20221213
LC record available at https://lccn.loc.gov/2022058944
LC ebook record available at https://lccn.loc.gov/2022058945

ISBN:   HB:      9781501346200
        PB:      9781501346194
        ePDF:    9781501346224
        eBook:   9781501346217

Typeset by RefineCatch Limited, Bungay, Suffolk
Printed and bound in Great Britain

Series: 33 1/3 Europe

To find out more about our authors and books visit www.bloomsbury.com
and sign up for our newsletters.

*To the musicians we have lost (2020–2023)*

# Contents

## Part 1  **Setting the Stage**

## Part 2  **Listening to *Amalia à l'Olympia***

# Acknowledgements

I am grateful to my series editor Fabian Holt for his enthusiasm and support and to Leah Babb-Rosenfeld and Rachel Moore at Bloomsbury for their editorial expertise. In Lisbon, José Carlos Alvarez, Maria Manuela Gomes dos Santos, and Sofia Patrão from the Museu Nacional do Teatro e da Dança granted me access to the museum archives and offered invaluable assistance. Frederico Santiago, tireless in all things Amália, generously shared resources from his private collection, conversation, and breathtaking moments of Amália listening. Ana Gonçalves did a rigorous read of the final version of the manuscript and gave thoughtful commentary. Lisbon's Valentim de Carvalho granted permission to reproduce the cover to the sheet music of "Mãe Preta" in Chapter 7 and the Biblioteca Nacional de Portugal provided a reproduction. Obrigada. My colleagues at Dickinson College provided warm collegiality. Ian Boucher and the staff at Dickinson's Waidner-Spahr library gave pandemic-era library support that went beyond the call of duty. Hanna Roman answered queries about my French translations. I thank an anonymous peer reviewer for astute feedback. Jessica Wood offered writing camaraderie and fielded my queries on the history of sound recording. David Looseley offered ideas on Olympia resources. I extend my gratitude to Dickinson College for their research and publication support and to the Bogliasco Foundation, their staff, and my fellow fellows, for their roles in facilitating the most ideal conditions possible in which to write the final part of this book. Steven Feld, welcomed me into his faculty seminar in intermediality sponsored by the Center for Experimental Ethnography at the University of Pennsylvania in the fall of 2020; I thank him and members Jairo Moreno, Eugene Lew, and Elyan Hill for their commentary at the early stage of this project. I also extend thanks to Louise Meintjes and her students, in her spring 2021 "On Recording" graduate seminar in anthropology at Duke University, for their feedback on an excerpt from the project. I presented portions of Chapters 1 and 9 at the conference "Musical Proximities," sponsored by the Canadian Society for Traditional Music in November 2021. Any errors or misrepresentations are my own.

*Amália at the Olympia* was created with the support of a Bogliasco Foundation Fellowship.

# Notes on the Text

I have written this book as a mosaic of sorts. Part I sets the stage for the album, presenting histories and contexts of performance, a biography of Amália's voice and a primer to the genre of *fado*. Part II zooms into specific tracks, guiding listening while telling backstories and social histories of the songs. Two interludes cut through the text, each providing alternative perspectives on mid-1950s Portugal, the first from a North Atlantic Treaty Organization (NATO) film, the second from Simone de Beauvoir's novel *The Mandarins*. Specific tracks in Part II, and the interludes, can be read in any order, but I suggest beginning with Part I.

The album issue that is the main subject for this book is the 33 1/3 "long play" record *Amalia à l'Olympia* (FSX 123) published in 1957 in France by Columbia (produced in Paris with Pathé Marconi).[1] Digitally remastered versions are available on multiple streaming services. Listening guide time stamps in the main text of the book correspond to versions of the album with fourteen tracks (where the first track contains both the voice of an announcer presenting Amália Rodrigues and the song "Uma Casa Portuguesa"). I link many recordings and performances in the notes. While reading, I invite you to pause to listen to specific moments in the album and to linger, to listen to other recordings I call out or to discover new ones, allowing your listening to permeate your experience of reading. Translations are mine unless otherwise indicated.

# Amalia à l'Olympia (1957) Track List

## Side A

1. Uma Casa Portuguesa (Reinaldo Ferreira; Vasco de Matos Sequeira, Artur Fonseca)
2. Nem às Paredes Confesso (Artur Ribeiro; Max, Ferrer Trindade)
3. Ai Mouraria (Amadeu do Vale; Frederico Valério)
4. Perseguição (Avelino de Sousa; Carlos da Maia)
5. Tudo Isto É Fado (Aníbal Nazaré; Fernando de Carvalho)
6. Fado Corrido (Linhares Barbosa; popular)
7. Barco Negro (David Mourão-Ferreira; Caco Velho, Piratini)

## Side B

1. Coimbra (José Galhardo; Raul Ferrão)
2. Sabe-se Lá (Silva Tavares; Frederico Valério)
3. A Tendinha (José Galhardo; Raul Ferrão)
4. Lá Vai Lisboa (Norberto de Araújo; Raul Ferrão)
5. Que Deus Me Perdoe (Silva Tavares; Frederico Valério)
6. Lisboa Antiga (José Galhardo, Amadeu do Vale; Raul Portela)
7. Amália (José Galhardo; Frederico Valério)

# Preface: A Yearning for Liveness

The album *Amalia à l'Olympia* (Amália at the Olympia) is a sound recording that bears witness to live events, to a run of performances in Paris in the spring of 1956.[1] I have written this book during a pandemic that has lasted over three years and claimed countless lives. Early on researchers discovered that aerosols, released with the breath that makes song, were capable of catalyzing heightened contagion. In the United States, opera houses and theaters were shuttered for over a year. In Lisbon, *fado* singers were unable to sing for live audiences.

Liveness, during that first year of the pandemic, took on the cast of something precarious, exotic, something historical, nostalgic, possible only in pre-pandemic times. It would be appropriate to use the Portuguese word *saudade* here, to indicate a deep longing for something (an experience, a person, a sensation, an object, a place) remembered in the past. In this context, the imaginary of liveness held aspiration and promise. We would know life had fully returned when we could attend a packed live performance with abandon, sitting shoulder-to-shoulder with strangers, reveling in sociality, reveling in presence.

## travel

*Amalia à l'Olympia* helped to launch Portugal's most internationally celebrated musical diva of the twentieth century and to bring the music of *fado* to listeners around the world. It functioned in its time as a kind of souvenir album that held the potential for international listeners, outside of Portugal, to stand in for Portugal while also standing in for cosmopolitanism, evoking the glamorous city of Paris, and presenting a voyage in sound. In the 1950s, Columbia Records in the USA would launch its "Adventures in Sound" series and Capitol records, its "Capitol of the World" series. Mid-Century "travel," or "holiday," albums, presenting virtual voyages in sound and music, were sometimes produced in collaboration with airlines (Borgerson and Schroeder 2017; Elliott 2014). The 1950s marked the burgeoning of international tourism and elite international commercial air travel; and albums like *Amalia à l'Olympia* call to be understood within this context.

In a year marked by enclosures, lockdowns, and stay in place orders, many yearned for movement, for travel. As I stayed in place, I tracked down different national releases of albums and the earlier recordings that led up to her Olympia engagement. I received missives from across the globe: slim white cardboard boxes, sometimes with a note on an enclosed card, all meticulously packaged, the vinyl record in clear plastic separated from its jacket, both jacket and record enclosed in thick sheets of cardboard. These LPs traveled to my front porch, in a small town in Pennsylvania, from a tiny record shop in Vermont, from a seller in California, from a vendor in Amersfoort in the Netherlands, and another in France. After a wait of many months, one day I found a Japanese release of her Olympia concert album on Odeon, in a box covered in twelve green, purple, and gold Russian stamps, outside my door. I carefully cut the tape, remove the vinyl record, set it on my turntable, spin it in motion brushing dust from the grooves, plug my headphones into the amp, place down the needle, and I listen.

There is her voice. There is the sound of people clapping, and Amália thanking her audience in French. There is her sense of drama; there are her long held *rubati;* there is her velvety full timbre and the tremendous swells in volume; and there are her *voltinhas*, the "little turns" of the voice that ornament key words and bring home powerful emotion. There are her luxurious slides into pitches from above and below; there is her animation and playfulness, the sweetness and the light ease and mastery in which she moves from one note to another, shaping a phrase, moving to the next. There are her wails, her cries, her translation of feeling into sound. Each album is a portal.

# PART 1

# Setting the Stage

PART 1

Setting the
Stage

# 1 Dresses, Acrobats, and the Sound of Moonlight

A dress of black silk damask swirled with dark black flowers. A cream-colored label inside, embroidered in gold with the mark of the maker, "R. Bianchi, Italia-Mexico" and a miniature crown. A narrow deep V at the throat, three-quarter-length sleeves, a dropped waist, darts on both sides. A zipper up the back. The dress is on a wooden hanger numbered 86863 in the National Museum of Theater and Dance, in a restored eighteenth-century palace in Lisbon. Amália Rodrigues, "the Queen of *Fado*," Portugal's most celebrated diva, likely wore this dress on stage in the 1950s.

Maria Manuela Gomes dos Santos hands me white gloves, spreading the dress across a table in the museum library in the summer of 2018. She points to different places on the dress. The V-neck and the dropped waist, she says, "helped to lend the illusion of length and of stature to Amália's physical presence on stage; it helped her gain a different physical dimension." She continues, "the V-neck also opened up the thorax"; she then turns the dress over to show me how the back is cut to allow for extra freedom and extension in the arms. *I think of the wrenching full-throated expressive force of the voice of Amália Rodrigues, its expansive register and dynamic range, and the breath behind the power of her sound and her characteristic wide-open-arms gesture at the end of some of her later filmed live performances and that I have seen imitated in drag.*

She slides the zipper down, it still works. She turns the fabric inside-out and reveals a small metal weight at the bottom of the V, explaining that the weight kept her cleavage from showing, in line with mid-1950s Portuguese mores around femininity. She points to a mark on the dress where the ribcage of Amália Rodrigues pushed up against the fabric as her lungs filled with breath that became voice, there is a pulling at the seams, noting, "She filled up the space there; if you look closely, you can see the puckering in the fabric at the waist that shows her true waistline, where the damask had doubled over." She reminds me that it was Amália who brought the custom of wearing black to the genre of fado, a practice that endures for fado performers to this day.[1]

There is a materiality of the memory of the body. Traces of embodied performance reside in the folds and creases of the fabric of this black silk, traces of breath, of movement, of voice. The creases of Amália's dress are a reminder that her recorded voice emanates from a living breathing body. The very material, living, breathing, sweating, performing, body is partially obscured by the sounds of her voice extracted and pressed into grooves on vinyl and amplified, the currency of the LP recording gaining added value and circulation through association with the cosmopolitan, prestigious, and strategically curated platform that was the Olympia Music Hall in its post-World War II revival.

In the recording, she becomes all voice, overwhelming voice in sound. The sounds on this LP—the voice of the presenter who introduces her, Amália's voice (sometimes briefly speaking [in French, in Portuguese], then singing in Portuguese), the sounds of her instrumentalists (one on the Portuguese guitar [*guitarra portuguesa*] with twelve steel strings strung in six double courses, one on the Spanish six string acoustic guitar [*viola*]), the edited applause, the occasional shout out from audience members—stand in as indices for the gestalt of multiple live performances that Amália Rodrigues gave at the Olympia over six weeks in Paris in the spring of 1956.

Listen to the last track on side A ("Barco Negro") of the 1957 LP made from her Olympia debut performances. Pay attention to the way she uses descending *glissandi* (sliding downwards between the pitches), to how she uses *rubati* (extending and drawing out the meter), and to her use of vocal ornamentation or *little turns* of the voice. I return to this song later in the book.

# Amália and the Olympia

The voice of Amália Rodrigues (1920–1999), Portugal's most celebrated diva, was extraordinary for its interpretive power, soul wrenching timbre, and international reach.[2] *Amalia à l'Olympia* (1957) is a recording culled from her first performances during two three-week runs at the fabled Olympia Music Hall in Paris in the spring of 1956. This album, reissued for multiple markets (including: USA, France, Italy, the Netherlands, Great Britain, South Africa, and Japan), catapulted her into the international limelight. The legendary stature of Amália Rodrigues in Portugal can be compared to that of Édith Piaf in France, Umm Kulthum in Egypt, Miriam Makeba in South Africa, Celia Cruz in Cuba, or Billy Holiday in the United States (all of whom incidentally performed at the Olympia in Paris). I use this album as a prism through which to explore interlinked processes and networks which shaped the internationalization of peripheral popular musics, the formation of cosmopolitan musical publics, and the performance of female vocal celebrity in the mid-twentieth century.

As a vocalist Rodrigues is principally recognized in the genre of fado. Fado emerged in the port city of Lisbon in the early 1800s as a form of urban sung poetry, with origin stories linked to Portuguese colonial expansion and Afro-Brazilian dance and musical forms (Portugal had colonies in Africa until the mid-1970s; the former colony of Brazil gained independence in 1822), to prostitution, criminality, and complaint. It is often associated with a sentiment of bittersweet nostalgia (a feeling which in Portuguese is known as *saudade*). By the mid-twentieth century, fado had been nationalized and censored by Portugal's dictatorial regime (1926–1974). In the final two decades of the Portuguese dictatorship, the voice of Amália Rodrigues traveled the world, on radio, in film, on vinyl records, and in extensive concert tours, as the "voice of Portugal." In addition to fado, Rodrigues is also celebrated for her genre and language-crossing prowess (she recorded in Italian, Spanish, English, and French), her roles in Portuguese cinema, and her skill as a poet. Her success in Portugal was shaped in relation to her international acclaim. While she had earlier performed at prestigious venues in the United States, Europe, and South America, and recorded for international markets, her 1956 Olympia debut and the 1957 album, made from her 1956 Olympia performances, helped to catalyze her enduring international success. This album marks a moment that prefigures fado's more recent (1990s–present) international prominence including: fado's 2011 designation by UNESCO as an "intangible cultural heritage of humanity," Lisbon's recent tourism-fueled fado boom, and particularly for female fado singers, the success of fado on the international market for world music. Fado's principal markets outside of Portugal, and opportunities for new female fado singers, have often been in places where Amália developed strong listening publics through the circulation of her recordings; the grooves and networks of circulation, listening, and genre endure.

The Olympia Music Hall, under the directorship and curatorship of Bruno Coquatrix, from 1954–1979, was key to the shaping of international musical stardom during the mid-twentieth century. Coquatrix was responsible for reviving the late nineteenth-century theater as a music hall in 1954 and internationalization was key to his mission.[3] To perform at the Olympia in Paris was, in a sense, to arrive. The importance of an Olympia debut would possibly be even greater for a performer from a country on Europe's periphery singing in a genre that was still not well understood outside of Portugal. At the same time, celebrity performers (or performers with the potential for high prestige) were the financial lifeblood of the Olympia in the mid-twentieth century.

The album is framed by Amália's rendition of a classic dictatorship-era song at the beginning, "Uma Casa Portuguesa" (A Portuguese house) and the fado song "Amália" at the end, one that casts her as the protagonist in the song, as diva of the genre of fado. Some of the repertoire included on this album would become central to her career. Many of these songs endure in the repertoire of contemporary fado musicians, and some continue to be covered and creatively reimagined in other languages and by non-Portuguese musicians. The live performances and the album played a key role in defining the genre of fado, in translating and framing it, and most importantly, in amplifying it for export for select mid-twentieth-century international markets and listeners.

Amália's first Olympia performances took place in April and May 1956. She first performed on the evening of April 10 at a farewell event for Josephine Baker. She subsequently performed in a three-week run from April 12–May 1, and then Bruno Coquatrix invited her back to perform in a rare second three-week run from May 3–22 with a different headliner act and line-up (Santos 2005 [1987], 120, 221). The resulting "live" album is edited; tracks were likely chosen from recordings of performances made on different days (Santiago 2020, 89). A critic who attended one of her 1956 Olympia performances mentions a song she sang in Spanish, "Los Cascabeles" (The Bells); another evening she sang the song "Vingança" (Revenge) by the Brazilian composer and singer Lupicínio Rodrigues.[4] Yet neither of these songs are included in the album. Frederico Santiago, who has worked on multiple projects of digital remastering of Amália's albums and recordings (including a 2020 re-edition of the 1957 Olympia album), notes that it is interesting that so many of the tracks (four) on the album have music composed by the Portuguese composer Frederico Valério; it would be unlikely that Rodrigues would have sung so much music by the same composer in one specific performance.[5] All fourteen tracks on the album are sung in Portuguese and with lyrics by Portuguese poets.

Much of the contextualizing information relating to the framing of the performance has not been included in album liner or sleeve notes; these omissions are sometimes mirrored in contemporary official museum exhibit commemorations in Portugal, which often leave out the full context for her debut performances while lauding the 1956 Olympia concerts in relation to the internationalization of her career. For example, Rodrigues' plaintive fado singing in her Olympia debut took place in the context of a Parisian *revue* (or vaudeville variety show). For the first three weeks, she appeared during the first half of the show, which also included a fabled British strongwoman, a Hungarian-Turkish dance duo, and aerial acrobats.

This book explores the role of Rodrigues' first Olympia performances (and the album which stands in for them) in shaping her stardom and the internationalization of the genre of fado. In so doing, I consider some of the following questions: (1) How does this album curate her voice? (2) What can we learn about the "live album" (or the sounds of the voice extracted and pressed into grooves) by decentering it, and shifting our attention to linked but peripheral objects (like a dress, a program, other recordings) that contain clues about her voice, the live performances and their framing, reception, and social histories? In other words, what might we learn about the history of the materiality of voicing and corporeal performance, by decentering the voice and the LP and examining peripheral (or abandoned) objects upon which sounding left its marks? (3) Lastly, what might close attention to this album and its social and performance histories reveal about the making of mid-twentieth-century female vocal celebrity?[6]

I contextualize her performance and the international reception of the recording of the performance within the frictions wrought by Portuguese dictatorship-era cultural policy and the mid-1950s internationalization of a local music (fado) from Europe's southwestern periphery via the conduit of the Olympia Music Hall in the city of Paris. Within these frames, I explore what internationalization looks and sounds like for this album, its afterlife, and for Amália's career. I do so by examining the traces and stories the album catalyzed or left behind, tracking some of the key networks in which the album traveled, and putting it in conversation with other material objects, sounds, voices, and histories to which it is linked. At every step, my exploration is shot through with acts of translation (as I read, as I examine objects, films, and photographs, as I listen, and as I write for you), translations between languages, the specificities of culture and historical moments, between media and formats, and between story, performance, and recorded sound.

# scrapbook

I sift through boxes of documents related to Amália's career in the 1950s at Portugal's National Museum of Theater and Dance. There are so many black-and-white photographs, some oxidizing, curling at the corners. There she is, over and over again, on the steps of an airplane on the tarmac (arriving, departing). Here she is in a Lisbon fado house, sometimes with her sister Celeste (who also sang fado) by her side; the names of the people in the photo written in by hand at the bottom. There she is, abroad, in Madrid, now Berlin, then Mexico, New York, and Paris. Here she is in her house in Lisbon (posed photo shoot) making her bed! Now in the laundry room wearing a white apron ironing a dress, her face perfectly made up. (*The celebrity does domestic things like all other women do.*) I feel a tenderness for her, all of this coming, all of this going, so much posing.

In these boxes, I find programs from her Olympia performance in the winter of 1957, when she would be invited by Bruno Coquatrix to return as the headliner main act, but nothing from her 1956 debut. When I finally track down a program, it is through a contact of the archivist at the museum, in the private collection of Frederico Santiago, carefully filed on his bookshelf, gifted to him by a contact of a Parisian Amália fan. Amália's handwritten signature runs across one of the pages; on the cover is neatly written on the top right corner: "30 Avril 1956."

# the program

(*first page*)

l'Olympia
*Votre* Music-Hall!
28, Boulevard des Capucines
Métro: Opéra – Madeleine
Téléphone: OPEra 47-20

*Représentations*:
(Performances)

*Tous les soirs à 20 h. 45*
(All evenings at 8:45pm)
*Matinées: Lundi, Jeudi*
*Samedi à 14 h. 45*
(Matinées: Monday, Thursday, Saturday at 2:45pm)
*Dimanche à 14 h. 30 et 17 h. 30*
(Sunday at 2:30pm and 5:30pm)
*Relâche le Mercredi*
(No performances on Wednesdays)

BRUNO COQUATRIX
*Directeur Général*

*PROGRAMME*
*du 12 Avril au 1 Mai*
April 12–May 1 [1956][7]

Imagine. It is a rainy night in Paris on April 30, 1956. You have your ticket for one of the final performances at the Olympia Music Hall in a three-week run headlining the French male singing group, Les Compagnons de la Chanson, who had been brought to fame by the French crooner Édith Piaf (a particularly famous hit featured the group accompanying Piaf in "Les Trois Cloches" [The Three Bells]). The theater has approximately 2,000 seats and you got the last seat available in the middle section of the front of the hall. The show would be a revue, a genre for which the Olympia was now known for, a variety show with multiple acts. You cue up with the crowds outside of the Olympia on the Boulevard des Capucines, and when the doors open, you shake off your umbrella, move inside, check your coat and purchase a program. You get settled in your seat and look around you; the hall is almost full. You eagerly begin to peruse the program.

The cover is all oranges, blacks, and browns featuring a detailed cartoon-like sketch of chaotic crowds as far as the eye can see along the Boulevard des Capucines and outside of the theater, waiting to get into the Olympia; a monkey parachutes into the scene diving headfirst from the sky, a man with a top hat in hand arrives on a horse, a woman in a black dress with her stocking garter exposed, sits on a moped near the front door, a bearded man climbs a ladder to adjust the marquee.

You ruffle through the pages, in addition to listings for the lineups for the first and second halves of the show, you find artist biographies, photos, and endorsements, advertisements for local restaurants, Coca-Cola, and the soda Amourette, and for a record, television, and radio store (Palais de la Radio et du Disque). You flip to the end, where you find pages of the latest news about new record releases on the labels of RCA, Pathé, Odéon, Decca, Barclay, and Columbia Records (for discs in 45 rpm [rotations per minute] and 33 1/3 rpm formats).

You read about the world premiere in Chicago in February of the film by Universal International Pictures, *The Benny Goodman Story* and read that now you can also see this in France! Even more, Decca records will soon release a 331/3 disc of the soundtrack of the film. You learn about a release of the number one hit song in the USA, "See You Later Alligator" (by Bill Haley and his Comets) and about a new record on RCA by the Canadian singer Guylaine Guy (who just had an "incredible run" in Brussels). You read that the Portuguese singer Amália Rodrigues (who will be featured in tonight's show), someone who is "no longer unknown to French fans of her songs and those accustomed to the dark rooms of the cinema," is releasing a record on Barclay with many popular fados (the disc announcement notes that fado contains "nostalgic accents" redolent of "the landscapes that surround [the Portuguese city of] Coimbra to the beaches around the coast of Porto"). Following all of the latest news about recordings is a small box with an image of a dog quizzically peering into the horn of a record player next to the words: "Sound in the hall of the Olympia is provided by His Master's Voice: production by Pathé Marconi."

## the first half

The French actress Monique Tanguy is listed as the presenter for the evening; next to her name is a small cut-out photo, perhaps Tanguy herself, of a young woman wearing a strapless leotard with a leopard print bodice and matching long gloves. The evening opens with Gaston Lapeyronnie, the Olympia house conductor and jazz trumpeter, directing his orchestra.[8] The Australian acrobats, The Six Flying De Pauls (referred to in the program as the "white kangaroos") are the first main act, followed by a "supplemental" performance by the French singer Geneviève Toussaint, noted in the program as "a headliner voice of the future with a face and figure of a pin up girl." Then comes the superstar British strongwoman Joan Rhodes (whom one can see in old television footage from the era bending metal with her teeth and ripping apart phone books with her bare hands, all while dressed in an evening gown) followed by an appearance by the French actor and singer Pierre-Jean Vaillard, and then the aerial acrobats Les Akeff will take the stage. (In an undated photo of Les Akeff from the French national library, one man lies on a bench with his right leg extended completely at a right angle to his torso, while the other man, stands on his head, his feet extending high into the air, his head balanced on the flat of the foot of the extended leg of the man lying on the bench; there is another photo in which the man lying on the bench has propelled the second man flying into the air, the photo catches the airborne man midflight, on a diagonal, arms straight at his sides.)[9] The Portuguese singer Amália Rodrigues will perform next (above her name in small font reads [translated from French], "the best interpreter of 'fados' whom we have ever heard"). The first half will end with performances by the sensational Hungarian/Turkish acrobatic ballroom dance duo Darvas and Julia. (An archival photo from a 1949 rehearsal in Lausanne shows Darvas standing, arms spread wide, with Julia horizontally suspended by muscular force, wrapped around his torso, her hands grasping her ankles.)[10] At the end of the listing in the program for the lineup of the first half, you read that during the interval you may visit the bar and have a smoke, and that some of the latest recordings made by the evening's stars will be available to purchase and for autograph.

# the program: endorsing Amália

In the middle of the program is a full page with the name "Maurice Carrère" in bold typeface at the top, followed by the words (also in bold type), "Everyone who has seen her sing, keeps the memory in their hearts of the beautiful AMALIA" (sic). The page is an extended endorsement for Amália by Maurice Carrère, the owner of the swanky nightclub Chez Carrère, near the Champs-Élysées, a club which was also a haunt of the singers Édith Piaf and Charles Aznavour.

The fact that Carrère comes with no introduction is likely testament to how well his name would have been known amongst Parisian audiences. In the words of the American photographer Marilyn Stafford, who was an expatriate in Paris in the 1950s, "[Chez Carrère] was the only club that Princess Elizabeth and Prince Philip had been permitted to attend while on an earlier visit to Paris."[11] "One evening at Chez Carrère I was invited to join Eleanor Roosevelt's table."[12] "There were Paris nightclubs, and there was Chez Carrère. It was the place to be."[13]

Carrère continues:

> Since it is the "Friends of the Olympia" who patronize this show, I claim the honor of presenting her to you. I became the most fervent admirer of this great artist the day … when she sang in Paris for a privileged few at my place near the Embassy of Portugal. She sang again in France in two galas that I organized in Biarritz, with Denise Tual.

He then compares Amália's stardom to that of Édith Piaf's, speculating that the art of Amália is perhaps "less international." He explains to the audience something about the Portuguese genre of *fado* and tells them that they will hear a song that they likely already know, a song called "Coimbra" which has already circulated on her recordings and is also known by the French title of "Avril au Portugal" [April in Portugal]).

> But I dreamed of having her acclaimed in Paris. It was difficult; Amália Rodrigues is a very big star. In Portugal and South America she is what Édith Piaf is to France and the United States, the biggest star. But her art, so simple and so subtle at the same time, is perhaps less … international [than Piaf's]. Because in her country, accompanied by her guitarists, she only sings "Fados." Fado is a love song, almost always melancholy and often heartbreaking, a kind of chant in which the dreamy soul of this apparently gay people is expressed. For Amália, the Olympia stage is not very intimate. But you will love at least one fado that you already know that was a triumphant success: [the fado named] *"Coimbra."* Coimbra: clear and mysterious, ancient and modern, this is the city of students. Under the title, "Avril au Portugal" [April in Portugal], "Coimbra," thanks to Amália Rodrigues, has toured the world.

In this endorsement, where Amália is being presented on the Olympia stage for the first time, Carrère renders her stardom and the genre of fado legible for the Olympia audience. The genre of fado is presented here for export as a "love song" and as "melancholy" and Rodrigues is framed as a fado singer, whose art is "simple" and "subtle." The framing in relation to Piaf is key; this serves as an example of one of the ways in which vocal celebrity in the mid-twentieth century is interdependently shaped (as celebrities are constituted *in relation* to one another), a point I return to at the end of this book.

The program is a dense document, a material object that provides a glimpse into (and evidence of) the multiple networks in which just one evening's show at the Olympia in the 1950s is embedded: networks of curatorship, of cultural capital and prestige, of relations between specific cities (including: Paris, New York, Hollywood), between sound recordings, films, live performances and their consumers. The program is a prism into aspiration laid bare (the making of stars), the desire to break through, of seeing and being seen, of listening and being heard. It is also a prism into and frame for pleasure, and it is charged with the aura of the city of Paris.

The printed Olympia program points to excess, a flooding or distraction of the senses. In the risqué framing of the program with photo cut outs of scantily clad women's bodies, and the language (one French singer is framed as having the "figure of a pin up girl") of sexualized objectification for the pleasure of the gaze, there is something vestigial of the Moulin Rouge or of the Olympia's earlier (1893–1920s) history ("with their sequined, feathered, and bare-breasted dancing girls" [Looseley 2015, 28]). The Olympia, when it re-opens in 1954 under the management of Bruno Coquatrix as a music hall, is a kind of variety act pleasure house of performance, where one form of consumption (for example, the live musical performance) prompts other forms of pleasure wrought through consumption (the pleasure of ownership of a recording, the pleasure of being cosmopolitan, the pleasure of listening as a cosmopolitan, the pleasure of being in the know about the latest musical trends, the pleasure of tourism). Listening to the periphery is framed in this context as a form of cosmopolitanism. At the same time, local specificity regarding this periphery is omitted (but rather referenced with stereotypes). In addition to the radical juxtaposition of performance forms, there is also the juxtaposition, combination, and inclusion of a multiplicity of places or nations as referenced through performers, who sometimes stand in as their icons. In the midst of this excess of variety, in between acts by aerial acrobats and by dancers, coming right after the acrobats Les Akeff, and followed by the dance duo Darvas and Julia, is Amália Rodrigues in her Paris Olympia debut. She is thirty-five years old.

## album cover (front)

On the cover of the French release of Amália Rodrigues' first Olympia LP (Columbia FSX 123) (1957) is a black-and-white photograph of Amália in the spring of 1956 on the Olympia stage. (The same photograph appears on the cover of this book.) Her head tilted slightly upwards with eyes half open, the photograph captures her in a moment of song, of focused attention, of expressive force. The Swiss-French photographer Sabine Weiss took this photo in her early thirties; she would become one of the most celebrated photographers of the twentieth century. She is known for her street photography and photojournalism, but also for her work in fashion photography, and for her portraits of musicians, artists, and writers. Igor Stravinsky, Benjamin Britten, Maria Callas, Pablo Casals, Ella Fitzgerald, and Charlie Parker were among her subjects.

Amália Rodrigues wears a long black dress, covered in black flowers, and a black shawl with a fringe over her shoulders and her arms; her hands come together clasping the fringe. Only her head, face, hands, and a small part of her neck are uncovered. Her dark hair merges with the darkness of the background. To her sides, and slightly behind her, are

Domingos Camarinha on the Portuguese guitar (guitarra) and Santos Moreira on the Spanish acoustic guitar (viola). Moreira gazes intently at Amália as she sings; Camarinha looks down to his right hand plucking the strings. The men are dressed in black suits and wear bow ties and cuff links. The three form a close triangle with Amália at the front; behind them is the dark of a black closed curtain of the Olympia stage. The blonde grain of the wood of the instruments and Amália's long glittering earrings, her face, and her hands catch the light.

## press clipping

Monday, April 23, 1956, *O Século* newspaper, Lisbon, front page

Headline: "In between a number by itinerant circus performers and another by acrobats, Amália Rodrigues delights Parisians (who consider fado a song of moonlight)."

There is a photograph of Amália Rodrigues wearing a black dress with embroidered black flowers on the Olympia stage in a review on the front page of the Portuguese newspaper *O Século*. Amália is framed by three microphones on stands. Around her right shoulder is wrapped a black shawl with a flowing fringe. On the same front page is an article about the seasickness suffered by the film star Grace Kelly when she crossed in a boat from Villefranche-sur-Mer to Mallorca and news about violent thunderstorms in Portugal over the past weekend, accompanied by hail.

The critic, Marcel Dany, purchases a program at the entrance and confesses surprise at finding Amália's performance, and the music of fado, positioned in between a number by acrobats, "although excellent," and a performance by itinerant circus performers (*saltimbancos*).

> Following energetic clangs of the cymbals and howls of the saxophone that accompanied the trio of aerial acrobats, a short silence fell, the curtain rose and a circle of strong light appeared, and in this circle, in the classic position, the fado singer [*fadista*], accompanied by two *guitarristas*, immobile and priestly … Magically, the voice and the *guitarras* transported the spirit far away from the noisy and rainy Boulevard des Capucines, far away from Paris, to a Portugal of memories, of *saudades* and of dreams [*sonho*], so much so, that I forgot to applaud, when the hall erupted in applause and cheers.

He describes four repeated shows over that weekend at the Olympia in which Amália appeared (Friday evening, Saturday matinee, Saturday and Sunday evening), observing different atmospheres and audiences, a large Portuguese-speaking audience on Friday night, an almost completely French audience on Saturday evening and a public on Sunday evening that was "more elegant" and composed of French, Portuguese, "Anglo-Saxons," and South Americans.

He describes the applause on the Friday evening, when there were the most Portuguese (Portuguese who lived in France) in the hall, as being most enthusiastic for the song "A Casa Portuguesa" (A Portuguese Home) and how on Saturday, with a mostly French audience, the song "Coimbra" received the most applause (noting that the song is known in France as "Abril em Portugal" [April in Portugal]) and that on the following Sunday evening, the song "Barco Negro" (Black Boat) received the most applause.

During the intervals, the critic eavesdropped on audience members as they exchanged impressions of the performance.

> Among the non-Portuguese spectators, many spoke with admiration about Amália Rodrigues and speculated about fado and the genre of song. In spite of their obvious admiration for the talent of the artist, some of the conceptions they had [about fado] would make the hair of those who frequent Lisbon's fado houses stand on end. They can be excused for this; there is their surprise at the originality of the genre and the fact that they have no knowledge at all of the language in which fado is sung.

The critic presses a young French woman to describe her reaction to the fados she had heard, she responds, "it [fado] seems to have something like moonlight in it."[14]

# dresses

I return to Lisbon in June 2022, my first visit since the start of the pandemic. I meet with Maria Manuela Gomes dos Santos, at the National Museum of Theater and Dance, to confirm some details about the dress that she had showed me in 2018. As I am reading my description, from the beginning of this chapter, out loud to her, translating from English to Portuguese, she stops me and tells me they have the dress that Amália likely wore at the Olympia. She leads me up a dimly lit flight of stairs, into a cramped loft under the rafters, above the library reading room. Rows of dresses hang on racks, covered in transparent mesh protective fabric; there is a table in the middle of the racks with an iron on it. She searches for her gloves and then pulls a long black silk dress embroidered with black flowers (numbered MDT 101407) from the rack.

It has three-quarter-length sleeves. There is deep V at the neck and a cut in the back that allows for extension in the arms. A dropped waist. There is a pronounced doubling in the fabric at the natural waist. We turn the dress inside out. There is a small metal weight at the bottom of the V, just like in the first dress, to keep the sides in place, to ensure modesty. We hang the two dresses side by side. They appear the same size, the first dress of black silk damask, the second of black embroidered silk, both with black flowers on black fabric. They are cut almost identically but the second is more lavish. I notice how long the dresses are. Maria Manuela reminds me how Amália was not a tall woman, that on stage she wore shoes with towering heels which would have been hidden under the hem of the dress, and how she would have likely also worn a crinoline under the dress, perhaps made from whalebone, to give the skirt more volume. I recognize the second dress from the photograph in Marcel Dany's critic's review from *O Século* from April 23, 1956 (above). To my eyes, the first dress, the one I saw in 2018, looks like the dress she wears, in the photograph by Sabine Weiss on the album cover of the 1957 French release, but I cannot be positive. She gave so many performances at the Olympia in that spring of 1956, she would have needed multiple stage dresses. There cannot be just *one* dress. We look at the zipper on the second dress (the one with black embroidered flowers). The puckering that we saw in the first dress, in the fabric alongside the zipper, is less pronounced, as the dress has been restored and the zipper replaced. I think about parallels, in the restoration of the dress, to sound recording as a historical document, about master recordings and copies, and about digital remasters. I think about the traces of the body and voice in what remains, in the fabric of her dresses, in the grooves etched into vinyl, in digitally remastered recordings of her voice, of what has been lost, of what endures. I think also about these two dresses in relation to repetition (the style, the color, the size, the cut) and of Amália's stage dresses as a genre. Manuela tells me about how Amália would refer to her dresses, as "as fardas de Amália" (the uniforms of Amália).[15] This second dress is like the first in the ways in which it plays with illusion and lends power (in the expansive cut in the back) to Amália's breath and her voice—the long hemline, the deep V at the neck, and the dropped waist designed to trick the eye, to maximize and to compliment the power of her voice, expanding the dimensions of her presence.

# 2  Biographies of Her Voice

Amália Rodrigues died on October 6, 1999. Portugal held three days of national mourning. On the day of her funeral, thousands thronged the streets outside of Lisbon's Basílica da Estrela, where her funeral was held, many singing her fados. She is the first woman to be buried in Portugal's National Pantheon (Gray 2013, 180). Since her death, her afterlife has continuously flourished in Portugal—in the repertoire and performance style of contemporary fado singers, in the attention given to the memorialization of her persona and her voice, and as part of the soundscape of the public sphere.[1] She expanded the limits of what was considered possible for female performers in Portugal, for fado singers, and for Portuguese musicians. In markets for fado or for Portuguese music in which she once dominated, she remains as the quintessential fado singer, leaving a legacy and a debt that emerging young fado artists, for the past two decades, have had to acknowledge, both at home and abroad.

The marks of the social and musical power of her voice, her life and her persona are writ into the contemporary landscape of the city Lisbon, in street murals, in graffiti, in the name of a park. Her former home on Lisbon's Rua de São Bento is now a museum. In response to increased attention to her memorialization, catalyzed by the centenary of her birth in 2020, new publications continue to emerge, some promising to reveal new biographical and political details or to keep her memory alive for Portuguese children.[2] New recordings, covers or homages by contemporary *fadistas* are released. Old unpublished reels are excavated and early recordings digitally remastered. Museum exhibits continue to be curated on her career. Her history of innovative, and sometimes controversial, artistry inspires younger generations, like the LGBTQ+ fado group, Fado Bicha, to forge their own paths. In 2021 the Portuguese Ministry of Culture decided to nominate recordings of Amália Rodrigues for consideration by UNESCO's documentary heritage program "Memory of the World."[3] In Paris, in 2010, the former square of the Boulevard d'Algérie, in the nineteenth *arrondissement*, was named in her honor; a blue sign with a green border, reads "Promenade Amalia Rodrigues: 1920–1999: *Chanteuse Portugaise.*"

# diva chronologies and geographies

I narrate aspects of the early decades of her career and public biography leading up to her 1956 Olympia debut, as they relate to the intertwining of the shaping of her celebrity, the internationalization of her voice and persona, and movement or circulation between key places (in person or on recordings). These details circulate publicly, presenting a continuously evolving public "biography of a voice" (Gray 2013, 185). In using the phrase "biography of a voice," I draw attention to the ways in which published biographical accounts, Amália's recorded performances and interviews, the lyrics which she sung (some of which she wrote herself), the talk of fans, popular press discourse and marketing, projects of memorialization, and the narratives of contemporary fado musicians about Amália, work in tandem, mapping fragments of biographical narratives onto the sound of her voice.

Much of the arc of the story of her life and the trajectory of her career has been and continues to be shaped by Amália herself, particularly through the circulation and citation of the book *Amália Uma Biografia,* written by Vítor Pavão dos Santos (2005 [1987]), the former director of Lisbon's National Museum of Theater and Dance, and a longtime fan of Rodrigues. In constructing the narrative, Santos draws on interviews he conducted with Amália between 1982–1986, prompting her reminiscences by a scrapbook of press clippings from her career that he had made. In the book, he omits the questions he asks her; the narrative reads as if it were an autobiography (but it is not).[4]

Amália Rodrigues was born in Lisbon in 1920.[5] She was raised in Lisbon, mostly by her grandparents and in poverty. Her parents were from the Beira-Baixa, a rural region northeast of Lisbon. After finishing primary school at twelve years old, she began working in various odd jobs; including selling fruit to Lisbon tourists and working in a cake factory. As a teenager, she sang in amateur fado settings and in her late teens, she began singing in Lisbon's professional fado houses (Nery 2010, 1133). Even in Lisbon, in the 1940s, her singing would reach a cosmopolitan, international clientele (Santiago 2020, 2). Lisbon, was a crossroads for many non-Portuguese during World War II, partially related to Portugal's "neutrality."

Rodrigues' first major international performance was in Madrid in 1943. In Madrid, she had contact with the genre of *flamenco*; she would later listen to recordings of the Spanish flamenco singer Lola Flores and begin to incorporate some flamenco into her early repertoire (Nery 2010, 1133). She performed for the first time in Brazil in 1944. She returned to Brazil for a ten-month engagement in 1945, making her first recordings in Rio de Janeiro (they were in the format of 78 rpm records).[6] Vítor Pavão dos Santos argues that these records, which appeared in Portugal the following year and were broadcast widely for many years on Portuguese radio, were thus instrumental within Portugal in enabling her voice reach a wide public (2005 [1987], 255). She would continue to return to Brazil throughout her career and in 1961 she married the Brazilian engineer César Seabra (Nery 2010, 1134). In her twenties she appeared in multiple musical-theater (*revista*) roles in Lisbon and in Rio de Janeiro and began acting, with singing roles, in films. Some of the songs that would become central to her repertoire were first heard in musical theater pieces or films in which she participated (including some on the 1957 Olympia album). In 1949, the Portuguese dictator António Salazar's minister of culture and director of propaganda, António Ferro, brought Amália to perform in Paris (at the Chez Carrère, Studio des Champs-Élysées, and at the Casa de Portugal) and in London (Santos 2005 [1987], 99, 220). After her first performances in Paris in 1949, a critic in the French press lauded her "inexhaustible breath which warms the ends of phrases and her singular timbre that no professor has sanded (*poncé*) or banalized with the *bel canto*."[7]

The first half of the 1950s were pivotal for the internationalization of her career on both sides of the Atlantic and for the shaping of her prestige and celebrity. She participated in the Marshall Plan concerts in Berlin, Paris, Dublin, and Bern in 1950 and performed in Mozambique and Angola (both Portuguese colonies at that time), and the Belgian Congo in the following year. In 1952, she recorded an album at the Abbey Road Studios in London and performed for the first time at the club La Vie en Rose in New York City, where she remained for a four-month engagement (Nery 2010, 1133).

In 1953 she performed in Mexico City and returned to the United States, appearing on NBC television's *Coke Time with Eddie Fisher* where she sang a version of the song "April in Portugal"/ "Coimbra" where she began singing in English and switched to Portuguese; she had met Fisher's agent while at La Vie en Rose in 1952 (Santos 2005 [1987], 103). Returning to the USA in 1954, she gave multiple performances at Hollywood's Mocambo nightclub and returned to New York City at La Vie en Rose, making her recording debut in the United States, with *Amalia Rodrigues Sings Fado from Portugal Flamenco from Spain*, with Angel records (Nery 2010, 1133).[8] Angel's introduction of Amália in their album announcement in their May 1954 bulletin notes her live club performances in both New York and Hollywood. Critic reviews excerpted from *The Billboard, Newsweek, Time,* and *The New Yorker* praise her voice and her dramatic presence and frame the genre of fado for an American (U.S.) audience.[9] Later that month, Angel Records would run a large advertisement in *The Billboard* promoting Amália's album *Amália Sings Fado from Portugal Flamenco from Spain,* declaring: "Fado is FASCINATING! Fado is THE FAD! What is fado? *House and Garden* calls it 'Portugal's own exotic form of the blues.'" A critic for *The Billboard* magazine notes on Angel Record's album advertisement: "It took 7 songs in a 20-minute stint to introduce Portugal's 'foremost singing star' to a movieland star-studded, first-night crowd at the Mocambo. But her opening, a gypsy song titled *Tani* was sufficient to establish Amalia Rodrigues in the firmament of elite vocalists."[10] (Note here the way in which the term "gypsy" is used as an exotifying adjective by the critic.)

On the other side of the Atlantic, the French film *Les Amants du Tage* (*The Lovers of the Tagus*) was completed in 1954 (the Tagus is the name of the river that runs through Lisbon). Directed by Henri Verneuil, it premiered in Paris, Lisbon, and London in 1955.[11] It was subsequently released in the United States as *The Lovers Net* and as *The Lovers of Lisbon*. Amália appears in the film in a secondary role as an owner of a fado house and as a fado singer. Fado songs, sung both by Amália and in orchestral arrangement, without voice, are used in the soundtrack. Images of city of Lisbon and touristic areas of Portugal, such as the traditional seaside fishing town of Nazaré, the genre of fado, and the voice of Amália are all sutured in the film, rendered for and made legible to a foreign (French) audience for touristic consumption (Baptista 2009, 66).

The music from the film would prove to have more enduring popularity than the film itself (Caille, 2009, 71). The songs "Barco Negro" (Black Boat) and "Solidão" (Loneliness), both from the soundtrack, are included on an album, with editions released in the USA, France, Portugal and the UK in 1955 (Santos 2005 [1987], 259).[12] Amália credits *Les Amants du Tage* for her international career, "The film launched me in France and France then launched me into the rest of the world. Previously, there had been [my performances in] America, but in Europe, they don't know what is going on there [in America]" (Santos 2005 [1987], 117). This comment likely refers to her perception regarding public sentiment about her rather than to the music and culture industry in the mid-1950s, in which postwar networks between New York and Paris played a key role in the formation of international musical celebrity.[13]

That the film led to her Olympia debut and that the Olympia debut to her international celebrity is the common narrative in the presentation of Amália's public biography and chronologies.

In these narratives, it is primarily through French cultural production and acclaim in France and Paris, rather than success in New York and Hollywood, that her celebrity is cemented. She points to the popularity of the song "Barco Negro" (following the film and the release of the LP containing songs from the film) for leading to her Olympia debut in 1956, "As 'Barco Negro' was being played all over France, they were interested in bringing me to the Olympia, that was during that time, a site that just to perform there, was already a consecration [consagração])" (Santos 2005 [1987], 119). "Barco Negro" would be included in her first Olympia concert and become a signature song in her repertoire.

She arrived in Paris on April 9, 1956, following an engagement in Brazil. On Tuesday evening, April 10, there was a large farewell party at the Olympia for the celebrated American-French performer Josephine Baker; it was decided that that was to be the occasion to present her to the French public and press. She sang only one song, a fado entitled "Confesso" (I Confess). She claims to have sung poorly, to be ashamed of how she sang, that she was nervous "singing in Portuguese, a language that no one knew, for an audiência snob [high-society audience] that was bidding farewell to a much-loved star, [singing] this [long] fado that went on forever" and that her "mouth was so dry that she could hardly speak." She recounts how much later she found out that Bruno Coquatrix had asked her agent in France, Félix Marouani, following her performance that evening, why he had brought Amália, "this girl who doesn't know how to sing" to perform at the Olympia as the vedette américaine (the performer who appears during the first half as a special guest prior to the main act) for the upcoming run (Santos 2005 [1987], 118, 119).

Bruno Coquatrix gave Amália Rodrigues another chance. Amália recounts that on Wednesdays (the one day of the week in which there were no performances at the Olympia) Coquatrix would hold an open rehearsal, with paid tickets, for the upcoming Olympia show, at the theater of Versailles. In rehearsal, audience applause determined decisions regarding cuts or substitutions [in the case of a singer, of repertoire] for the Olympia show. Amália claims that the audience liked her so much during that rehearsal [on April 11] that Coquatrix embraced her, saying, "A triumph! Amália, if you wish … you will be the biggest star in France" (Santos 2005 [1987], 120).

The three-week run at the Olympia opened the next day, Thursday, April 12, 1956, with the *Les Compagnons de la Chanson* as the main act. When that run completed, Coquatrix broke with precedent and asked her back for the next show, still in the role of *vedette américaine*, with the French comedian Fernand Raynaud as the headliner act. Amália accepted his offer. By her account and that of the French press, her Olympia performances during those six weeks were a dazzling success (Santos 2005 [1987], 121; Santiago 2020, 41, 42).

Coquatrix invited her back again to perform at the Olympia the next winter, this time as the main act. She states, "The following year [1957], I returned to the Olympia as the star of the show and after this it never stopped. It was crazy!" (Santos 2005 [1987], 121). She would return to perform at the Olympia in 1959, 1960, 1967, 1972, 1973, 1975, 1985, 1987, 1989, and 1992 (Santiago 2020, 9–19). In the late 1950s, she would sign a recording contract with the French label Ducretet-Thomson and Bruno Coquatrix would volunteer to open up a fado house for her in Paris. In 1958, Ducretet-Thomson would release a 45 EP of Amália singing in French.[14]

She never took Coquatrix up on his offer of a French fado house. But to Paris, she would return again and again. She would accept engagements at other prestigious Parisian venues (including Bobino, ABC, and La Tête de l'Art) and perform widely in France throughout her career. In 1959 she received the Médaille de la Ville de Paris (The Medal of the City of Paris). Looking back on her career, Amália commented, "Because of Paris, I went to Japan, to Russia, to the Arab countries, to Scandinavia, to Israel, the Netherlands, and Italy. Without Paris, I would have never had this international career" (Santos 2005 [1987], 121–128).

At the same time, her success in Paris brought prestige and diplomatic opportunities to Portugal. Her first Olympia concert was followed in June 1956 in Lisbon by a special reception in her honor which included "ambassadors, artists, writers, and politicians."[15] The debut concerts of Amália Rodrigues at the Olympia in 1956, and the LP that stands in for those concerts, played a key role in both defining the Portuguese musical-poetic genre of *fado* and linking fado to the place of Portugal and to the voice and persona of Amália Rodrigues for international listeners.

# 3  A *Fado* Primer

## histories

Fado, which translates literally as "fate," developed in Lisbon in early decades of the 1800s as sung poetry voiced from the city's margins, from its brothels, its prisons, its hardscrabble working-class neighborhoods, from its dispossessed.[1] It rapidly gained favor amongst the more well-to-do and elites and traversed multiple strata of Lisbon society. Fado reflects a convergence of multiple influences and styles, most likely Afro-Brazilian, European, and regional Portuguese. While fado's origins still remain fiercely contested by many fado musicians and fans in Portugal, scholars make persuasive arguments for its hybrid roots, particularly for the influence of Afro-Brazilian musical and dance forms the *fofa* and the *lundum* and from a form of fado that was danced in Brazil. When Napoleon's troops invaded Portugal in 1807, members of the Portuguese royal court fled to Brazil, bringing many with them and temporarily settling in Rio de Janeiro; the number of people who fled Portugal, may have been as high as 14,000 (Nery 2012, 53). The Portuguese court remained in Brazil for over a decade, and when they returned, they brought musical and dance styles back with them to Lisbon (Tinhorão 1994). The development of fado was likely also influenced by the song genre of the *modinha* which circulated in Brazil and then became popular in Lisbon (Nery 2004).

In the later decades of the 1800s, fado also featured prominently in Portuguese vaudeville shows known as *revista*, and in the early 1900s, workers creatively used fado as a form of protest (known as "workers' fado" or *fado operário*). During Portugal's long dictatorship (1926–1974) fado was professionalized and censored; official *casas de fado* (fado houses) opened which were monitored, in which fado singers (*fadistas*) and instrumentalists were paid, while some fado musicians and poets continued to clandestinely sing and write fado, that critiqued the regime. Fado was broadcast on state-controlled radio, featured as the soundtrack of Portugal's first sound film in 1931 and circulated internationally, particularly in the later decades of the regime in the voice of Amália, as the "voice of Portugal." Fado fell out of favor for many Portuguese on the political left after the fall of the regime in 1974 but was revived internationally in the early 1990s with the rise of markets for "world music." The largest concentration of fado venues and performance scenes remains in Lisbon. Fado in contemporary Lisbon is performed in a vast array of venues and contexts, from concert-hall stages, to small working-class bars, to tourist-oriented fado restaurants and clubs, to upscale casas de fado, and street and neighborhood festivals; prior to the 2020 pandemic, both amateur and professional scenes were thriving.

While fado's roots are intercultural and hybrid, and even though contemporary Portugal is highly multicultural and ethnically, racially, and linguistically diverse, the majority of Portuguese listeners and performers are white Portuguese, with a wide spectrum with regard to social class. Fado is also performed in other Portuguese regions and cities (for example, the Algarve and Porto) and in Portuguese communities in multiple parts of the world.[2] Fado currently may be experiencing a new golden age, with many Portuguese young people interested in singing and learning to play the *guitarra*, with vibrant and diverse local professional and amateur scenes thriving in Lisbon, and with many stars, particularly women, on the international stage.[3]

# practices

Fado is customarily sung by one singer (male or female), called a *fadista*, and accompanied by one or two instrumentalists on the Portuguese guitar (*guitarra portuguesa)* and by another instrumentalist on the six-string Spanish acoustic guitar (*viola*). Sometimes a bass guitar or (less common) a stand-up bass joins. Fado instrumentalists are almost always male. The guitarra and viola improvise "in dialogue" (Castelo-Branco 1994) with the fadista and the bass line of the viola provides the harmonic and rhythmic grounding and propels the rhythm forward (Gray 2013, 140). The guitarra, with twelve steel strings strung in six double courses, and plucked with fingernail extensions, is the defining instrument of fado sound, known for its shimmering, harpsichord like timbre and for its expressive power, at times almost approximating the human voice. Some of the words that fado musicians and listeners use to describe the techniques and sounds of guitarra playing reflect this likening of the instrument to the human voice. Fado lyrics might describe a guitarra that sings (*cantar*) or that sobs (*soluçar*) (Gray 2013, 140) and some lyrics gender the instrument as female. Fado is a genre of the night, traditionally, when sung in intimate venues, is performed in semi-darkness with candles on the tables or a dim lamp in the space. The darkness helps to direct the attention of the listeners to the sound of the voice, and inwards, to the realm of feeling. While fado has origins in dance, in contemporary performance, fadistas are often remarkably still, feet firmly planted, grounded to the floor, head thrown back, eyes closed: sometimes they might sway a bit from side to side, sometimes using the hands and arms to gesture, sometimes with an almost complete stillness in the body with the exception of the movement of breath and sound, and dramatic facial expression while singing.

Fado performance links story, life experience, emotional expression, musical improvisation, creativity and interaction, and poetry. Many fado musicians learn to sing and to play through traditions and practices that are passed down orally, historically in small venues where amateurs gathered to sing or in professional casas de fado. Listeners also learn how to listen to fado in these contexts. Fado recordings also serve as a pedagogical resource for learning how to sing and to play fado instruments, and also for listeners to cultivate knowledge of fado repertoire (Gray 2013, 53–55).

# forms

Fado musicians, listeners, and poets often differentiate the two primary sub-genres of *fado tradicional or fado castiço* (traditional fado or "authentic fado") from *fado-canção* (lit. fado song). Traditional fado is strophic, meaning that each stanza of the poem contains the same basic underlying melodic, harmonic, and rhythmic structure. Traditional fado forms can infinitely accommodate new poems; any given traditional fado form can be set with different lyrics, as long as the poem has the right number of lines (and sometimes syllables) for the specific fado form.

Musically, improvisation is particularly foregrounded in fado tradicional (traditional fado) in which instrumentalists and fadista improvise on set musical bases passed down through oral tradition. Traditional fado musical bases are distinguished by particular harmonic and melodic configurations but melody is often highly improvised. There are hundreds of these musical bases, but far fewer (under 100) are performed in routine practice. In traditional fado, because tunes can so easily accommodate new lyrics, iterations of fado poems previously set to the same melodic-harmonic structure of any given traditional fado form, can linger as a kind of affective residue which may color the hearing of subsequent fados with the same structure. For the seasoned listener, one hearing of a traditional fado with one set of lyrics, sung by a particular artist, can become stacked on top of previous hearings of the same traditional fado structure, sung perhaps with different lyrics and by a different artist. I have written about this kind of listening prompted by traditional fado, where traditional fado form serves as a kind of auditory palimpsest, as "cumulative listening" (Gray 2013, 156).[4]

In traditional fado, a premium is placed on the originality of the singer's musical improvisations and the improvisations of the instrumentalists in relation to the voice. Improvisatory melodic and ornamental vocal styling (*estilar*) and the manner in which the fadista divides the syllables of the poem and 'speaks' the words of the poem and expresses feeling, are held in high regard by many listeners. Technologies of sound recording for fado in the early twentieth century forever changed the length of traditional fado, forcing a time limit (thus dramatically curtailing the number of verses) so that fados could fit on a wax cylinder or on the side of a 78 rpm record, thus shifting traditional fado away from narrative chronicle in sung poetry to a more compact poetic/musical form (Nery 2012, 282).

Fado song (fado-canção), which emerged from musical theater (*revista*) beginning in the late 1800s and was later amplified through the film industry, often contains refrains, is not strophic, and the lyrics and tunes normally travel together. In fado-canção, the singer usually has less improvisatory leeway. A suggestion given by the musicologist Rui Vieira Nery, to translate how fado-canção works, to an international audience, is to think of the song "Night and Day" by Cole Porter; while it has been covered by many, we associate that melody with specific lyrics.[5] It is the same with fado-canção or "fado song"; melodies of fado-canção are attached to specific lyrics. In practice, however, there is some fluidity in how this works (Castelo-Branco 1994) as poets, borrowing from the practice in traditional fado, occasionally write new lyrics for existing fado-canção (Gray 2013, 17).

With both fado-canção and traditional fado, listeners and singers value the fadista's originality of repertoire, vocal style and timbre (tone color), and the ability to sing "from the heart," to "sing with soul" (*com alma*), to move others with their singing, and to persuasively sing lyrics that reflect the fadista's lived experience. In cases where young children sing tragic fado lyrics about romantic love and loss, this might be criticized as being inappropriate (Gray 2013, 214). Likewise, if someone from a wealthy family were to sing a fado lamenting the injustices and hardships of poverty, this might be criticized by some listeners as being in bad taste. While originality of repertoire and choice of lyrics is perhaps less important in the current moment than it was in the mid-twentieth century, during the time of Amália's career, originality of repertoire was one of *the* distinguishing hallmarks of a "true" fadista. Then, as today, poets sometimes write specifically for the voice of a particular fadista.

Fado poetry, over the history of the genre, has covered a vast range of themes, including the city of Lisbon and its neighborhoods; the travails of romantic love; loneliness;

abandonment; love for one's mother or father; Portugal's colonial "discoveries"; the sea; and perhaps most of all, a sentiment of *saudade*, or a bittersweet nostalgia. As in the genre of the blues, many fado lyrics are reflexive, about the genre itself. These fados comment on some aspect of the genre of fado (the sound and sentiment of the guitarra; fadistas, instrumentalists, and venues in the past; the emotion or sound in a singing voice; the relationship of the genre to feeling and to places within the city of Lisbon). Not all fado's are sad, saudade-filled or tragic; a fado poem might be humorous, upbeat, or even raunchy. While the scope of topics for fado lyrics is potentially without limit, and while fado has a long history of social critique, and poets continue to innovate on new themes, the years of censorship under the dictatorship, left its mark on fado lyrics, even in terms of lyrics which are commonly performed in the twenty-first century (Gray 2011).

During the later decades of the regime, the state increasingly appropriated fado as Portugal's national song form and simultaneously promoted it in relation to Portuguese tourism. Along with the Catholic church, fado served as one of three cultural pillars that bolstered the regime (fado, football, and the cult of the Saint of Fatima), sometimes referred to by Portuguese as simply as "the three Fs." In the final decades of the regime, fado lyrics shifted more and more toward themes of saudade, romantic love, and fatalistic loss and away from expression of individual suffering, life story, or anything that might be read as critique of the regime (Nery 2004, 192). This tendency is reflected in the repertoire included in Amália Rodrigues' 1957 Olympia album. Under censorship, lyrics proliferated that celebrated Portugal, the city of Lisbon and its quintessential fado neighborhoods, and Portuguese colonialism through a sentimental and romantic gaze. Some of these lyrics teach moral lessons, sometimes romanticizing poverty, extolling the moral virtues of humility and the nuclear family. Many lyrics from this period also implicitly or explicitly teach lessons about gender, about how to be or feel properly feminine or masculine, woman or man, and what sentiments are appropriate in heterosexual romantic love. As a diverse and powerfully expressive poetic and musical genre that spanned multiple social strata while retaining deep roots in the working class, fado existed in a slippery and ambivalent relation to the state. While the dictatorship did much to control fado, censor it, and shape its message, some fado musicians and poets continued to sing and write fado, behind closed doors, that escaped the censors and critiqued ideologies and practices of the regime, sometimes singing and writing lyrics that listeners would understand by listening "in between the lines" (*entrelinhas*) (Gray 2013, 90).

# listening

A popular fado maxim states that a fadista is not just one who sings, but one who also knows how to listen to the fado (Gray 2007, 126). Fado listening, in the context of the live performance, in a dedicated fado venue with knowledgeable listeners, is highly participatory and social, done in silence, with rapt attention, sometimes with eyes closed. Listeners might silently move their lips to the lyrics of fados being sung. Sometimes, at key moments in the fado, listeners might shout out phrases to show their appreciation (for example, *garganta linda* [beautiful throat], *boa* [good], *ah fadista* [you are a true fadista]) [Gray 2007, 116]). But fado listening practices also vary greatly depending on context. In a venue that hosts regular amateur sessions, many "audience" members may also be singers, waiting their turn to sing; they might be intimately familiar with the repertoire of most of the fadistas present, noticing minute differences in performances from week to week. In expensive *casas de fado*, many of which cater primarily to a touristic clientele, and have a fixed group of paid fadistas, or in fado restaurants and amateur venues that have a constantly changing stream of tourists, the majority of listeners present, may not understand the meaning of the words being sung, or abide by tacit rules enforcing silent listening. As sung poetry, fado is highly dependent on listener's ability to understand the words being sung. Transmission is also dependent on the listeners' understandings of culturally, place-based, and historically specific references (which even among communities of Lisbon-based aficionados, might vary according to social class or generation). When fado performance is recontextualized, to an international concert hall or when the audience is comprised of mostly non-Portuguese, in order to render fado more legible, fadistas might change aspects of their performances to communicate to this audience (for example, use more bodily gesture, dance on stage, try to explicitly include the audience by asking them to hum a refrain or to clap, include short song summaries in the dominant language of the listeners, or choose repertoire that they think will transmit more readily to non-Portuguese speakers).

# crying icons

Multiple popular song forms and voiced lament genres around the world utilize vocal "icons of crying" which can have the effect of drawing the listener into the emotional world of the song or the lament through an emotional-kinesthetic empathy (country music is one of these genres, the Japanese *enka* is another [Fox 2004; Yano 2002]). The anthropologist Greg Urban has identified some of these crying icons as including "the cry break, the voiced inhalation, the creaky voice, and the falsetto vowel" (Urban 1991, 156). Fado style is replete with crying icons, including some not identified by Urban. One crying icon commonly heard in fado is a version of Urban's "falsetto vowel;" a male or female fado singer might use extended melismatic vocal ornamentation (singing many pitches on just one syllable) in their higher register (for a man in true falsetto, for a woman in the higher range of her natural vocal register). Some fadistas refer to this practice, of using melismatic ornamentation in a higher register, often at lower volume, with the term *pianinhos*.[6] Others include variations of descending vocal slides (*portamento, glissando*) or a tremulous or wavering voice sometimes employing a wide vibrato or held to the limit of breath (Gray 2007).[7] A fadista might use these styles when singing words or phrases that convey sentiments of loss, of deep sadness, of grief. Fado lyrics and iconographies are replete with references to crying. The word for vibrato on the Portuguese guitar is *gemido*, from the verb *gemer* (to weep) and just like the guitarra can weep or cry, the voice in fado lyrics is sometimes referred to as a "crying voice." The guitarra from Coimbra, which is often used to accompany Lisbon fado, even has the wooden icon of a tear on its scroll. If a listener is moved by a performance, it would be a compliment to say to the fadista, "your singing made me cry" (Gray 2007, 117).

# Amália as fadista

*How might we understand relationships between a musical genre, its histories, practices, and forms, and its most acclaimed diva?*

While for many, the voice of Amália stands in for the genre of fado, Amália was not a typical fadista. Admirers in Portugal often note that she was not "merely" a fadista, rather that she was also an *artista*, that she, through her unique vocal timbre, her musicality, celebrity, artistic and repertoire choices, her stage presence and international audiblity transcended the local specificity and performative and vernacular conventions of the genre of fado, thus transforming it (Gray 2013, 206).

From early in her recording and international career, she included non-Portuguese repertoire in her concerts; while already in the 1940s, she had begun incorporating Spanish flamenco, she would ultimately broaden her repertoire even further, singing not only in Portuguese and Spanish, but in French, Italian and English across multiple genres (including Broadway hit tunes, Mexican *rancheras*, Portuguese folk music and popular marches, Brazilian popular song, Italian folk songs).

Through her singing style, and her musical collaborations, her performance choices on the stage and in recordings, and her choices of fado texts she also vastly expanded the limits and possibilities within the genre of fado itself. In the 1960s she would begin setting high poetry to fado (including the Portuguese Renaissance poet Luís de Camões). This move was met with national controversy, as vernacular poetry was more common in fado and the genre of fado was seen by some as not suitable for the work of such an erudite poet. In relation to this controversy, in a nationally televised mock court hearing in 1965, she was interrogated by two suited men, one with a gavel, and responded to questions sent in by the public in a "court of public opinion." She was asked if her success on international stages had led her to abandon the true roots of "authentic" fado. Her reply, "I don't understand what people mean when they speak about 'authentic fado.' I believe that the people who sing must be authentic … and I do have this capacity to be authentic and sincere."[8] Her collaborations with the French-Portuguese composer Alain Oulman, expanded the poetic, musical, and harmonic language of fado; some of this work is featured in one of the most magnificent albums of the twentieth century by a Portuguese artist, *Com Que Voz* (With What Voice).[9]

# **4** Listening to Amália

You will hear Amália style and inflect words and notes, lending them heightened feeling. She might draw out a note (*rubato*), extending the meter, just when you think the phrase might end, holding it just a bit longer. You might pay attention to the ways in which she slides into notes from below the pitch or above. You might hear her change the timbre or color of a note or a phrase, moving perhaps from sweet to raspy, from bright to dark (and back again). On a particularly expressive word or phrase, you may hear Amália use extended melismatic vocal ornamentation, drawing out one syllable over many pitches, sometimes sounding almost microtonal, or using pitches that occasionally move between the half steps of the diatonic scale (imagine what the notes in between the keys of the piano would sound like). Fado practitioners and listeners sometimes refer to these ornaments with the word *voltinhas* (little turns). You might hear her use a wavering vibrato, sounding almost like a wail or a sob. You might hear sudden and dramatic swells in volume or sudden shifts in timbre. In addition to her mode of melismatic vocal ornamentation, these are some of the ways in which Amália cries in song and lends feeling and drama to the stories she sings. And if you listen to the same song sung by Amália recorded on/in different days, months, or years, each rendering will be different (sometimes markedly) reflecting her musical choices and those of her instrumentalists, and the creativity and art of her improvisation and vocal styling, the timbral changes in her voice as she ages and she evolves artistically. This ability to "style" a fado anew each time, even over a lifetime of performances of the same fado, is considered by many in Lisbon's fado worlds to be a hallmark of a true fado singer.

Fans have marveled to me at the uniqueness and extraordinary expressivity of her vocal sound and timbral changes in her voice throughout her career, noting how much pleasure they have in listening to the same song recorded by Amália at different stages of her life, hearing experience and age in the sound of her voice (Gray 2013, 205). Rui Vieira Nery understands the changes in her sound as belonging to three distinct phases of her career marked by different tessituras (or vocal registers):

> through the 1950s as a soprano, with the virtuosic use of ornamentation in her high register … later in full maturity until the beginning of the 1980s, as a mezzo-soprano marked by a thicker [*mais espesso*] and more velvety [*mais aveludado*] timbre with a characteristic "grain," … and by the final decade of her career, almost a contralto register … using the wide vibrato that was beginning to affect her [voice] as an additional factor [to add] dramatic emphasis.
>
> 2010, 1136

Nery writes about her techniques of vocal production and placement of the voice however as "relatively constant" throughout her career, and "close to styles of vocal production in other popular traditions of Mediterranean [sung] vocality" (he characterizes this vocal placement as back [*recuada*] and low [*baixa*] with the help of the throat "but never forced," with the use of ample legato in the connection of vowel sounds) (2010, 136).

I hear in her voice, throughout the scope of her recorded career, a sound, a timbre that is singular in the world of fado. This difference is marked in relation to many of the voices I have heard in Lisbon's amateur fado worlds, in which specifically female singers which I have heard of her generation (and younger) sometimes used a vocal placement which emphasized nasality. This is not to say that other mid-twentieth-century professional fadistas of the era had "nasal" sounds, but rather to speculate that more vernacular nasal sounds might not have been privileged by the recording industry.

In her earliest recordings made in Brazil in 1945, I hear a supple sweetness and fluidity in her sound and style. Already by the mid 1950s I hear more timbral depth (to use a visual metaphor, "darkness"), a quality that would greatly intensify moving into the 1960s and 1970s. By the very end of her career, when her voice has further dropped in register, there is a profundity, and an almost gravelly texture in her sound (an example would be her voice in her 1990 *Live in New York* [Town Hall] album).[1] Her musical inventiveness and creativity of vocal styling and expressivity, in relation to conveying the sentiments of the words of the poems she sang, continued to flourish and develop through to the very end. The timing of her Olympia debut was fortuitous in relation to the development of her voice and her artistry. These performances, the album, and the subsequent Olympia concerts in 1957 and 1959, that her wildly successful debut made possible, would launch her into her vocal and artistic prime of the 1960s. In the Olympia album can be heard promises of what her voice would soon become.

# "fado" at the Olympia and Amália as fado

When reflecting on her first Olympia performances from the 1950s, Rodrigues noted that fado "travels very poorly" and that she didn't know how she managed to bring it to an [international] audience outside of Portugal. Demonstrating savviness and intentionality in relation to repertoire choice and programming for an international (and non-Portuguese speaking) audience, she explains how she would alternate different kinds of repertoire and how she would present it:

> No one can bear to hear heavy fados for two hours in a language that they don't understand. After a certain point, they all start to sound the same. In France, as in any other foreign country, I sing a light fado, then a fado that is "more fado" [*mais fado*], later, some music that is more lively ... then another serious fado, then a Spanish song, then something else sad. When I present [to the audience], I say only the names of the songs; I don't say whether [the song] is in Spanish, Portuguese or Italian. *For the French, they were all fados* (emphasis mine).

Santos 2005 [187], 125

While all the songs that made it onto her 1957 Olympia album have lyrics by Portuguese authors, not all began their musical lives as fados (for example, "Barco Negro") or fit into the genre of Lisbon fado (for example, the song "Coimbra"). The majority of the songs on this album are in the genre of fado-canção (or fado "song"), the subgenre of Lisbon fado that some practitioners and Portuguese fado aficionados consider as "less fado," than the strophic, highly improvised form of traditional fado (*fado tradicional*), which some consider as *mais fado* (more fado) or as *fado fado* (Gray 2013, 67). When Amália, in talking about programming (above), says, "I sing a light fado, then a fado that is 'more fado' [mais fado]," this is the understanding of fado that she is referring to. Two examples of traditional fado on the Olympia album are "Perseguição" (Pursuit) and "Fado Corrido" (the name of one of the earliest traditional fado forms, literally meaning, "running fado").[2] Two of the many examples of fado-canção on this album are "Ai Mouraria" (Mouraria is an historic Lisbon neighborhood) and "Que Deus Me Perdoe" (May God Forgive Me).

When I began researching fado in the early 2000s, and was learning how to sing fado, some practitioners told me that the subgenre of "fado song" was *mais musicado*. It is challenging to precisely translate "mais musicado" into English, but the gist of this argument is that "fado song" is perhaps transmitted more by "the music," and the musical lyricism of the vocal interpretation, than in traditional fado (Gray 2013, 67). Whereas the successful transmission of traditional fado depends for the fadista on a fine-tuned art regarding diction (*dizer bem as palavras* [to say the words well]), the division of syllables of the words, and improvisatory skill honed by deep knowledge and practice with traditional fado forms (both as a listener and as a fadista). Powerful transmission of traditional fado also depends on the familiarity of the listener with conventions and forms of the genre and the ability to understand the words being sung along with their place-based, historical, and culturally specific references. As a foreigner, some fado musicians and listeners encouraged me to sing fado song rather than traditional fado. That the Olympia album contains far more fado-canção than traditional fado possibly reflects not only Amália's preference, but a wider idea that fado song was more likely to be musically legible by a foreign audience, than was traditional fado. "Fado song" would become *the* type of fado for international export.

# fado-fication: exporting Portugal, exporting Amália

Amália's statement, "for the French, they were all fados," even if she sang Italian or Spanish songs, points to the way in which the sound and style of Amália's voice for some listeners became emblematic of fado, whether what she sang was fado or not. This equivalency of fado to the voice and personality of Amália Rodrigues in France began with her first performances there in 1949 (Santiago 2020, 30). These links were made and a definition of fado for export was heightened through the ways in which she and fado were first presented to the Olympia public (as in Carrère's endorsement in the program notes), through films such as *Les Amants du Tage*, and the soundtrack recording that followed, in the popular press, and in the ways in which fado and Amália were represented on the album jackets of multiple international releases of the Olympia album. Whereas in the United States, Amália had initially been promoted as a singer of Iberian music (in the genres of both flamenco and of fado), the Olympia album links her firmly to Portugal and to fado.

Writing about the film *Les Amants du Tage*, the film scholar Tiago Baptista, observes that Amália (and fado) serves as a "tourist attraction" for the two protagonists in the film, ill-fated French lovers who are on holiday in Portugal (2009, 65). He argues that this framing is no accident, as it is precisely during the mid-1950s that fado venues in Portugal increasingly rely on tourist revenue as other forms of popular entertainment in Portugal become more inexpensive (Baptista 2009, 66). It is also during the 1950s that fado tourism is increasingly promoted by the Portuguese state as the censored genre is increasingly functioning as one of the pillars of the regime and professional fado performance, in state-sanctioned fado houses, is increasingly folkorized (Baptista 2009, 66; Nery 2004, 228). Baptista argues the film sutures a particular rendering of the genre of fado and "a sentiment of fatalism" to Amália and that she becomes a "living symbol of fado" (2009, 64, 74). The film uses Amália, her role in the film and the setting (a rendition of a Portuguese fado house replete with folkloric decoration) in which she sings, to render the genre of fado legible "for a public not familiar with fado," to frame it for foreign export, or tourist consumption, while at the same time, invoking "cultural cliches of Portugal" like "fado, the sea, saudade, etc." He notes similar touristic-driven Portugal-fado-Amália exoticisms in the 1955 British short film, *April in Portugal* (directed by Euan Lloyd), in which Amália also featured (Baptista 2009, 66).

These same "cultural cliches" invoked in *Les Amants du Tage* continue in the presentation of the 1957 Olympia album for the French public as versions of fado, Portugal, and Amália for export are explicitly linked in promotional language used on the back of the album. The back jacket of the French release contains an extended endorsement and introduction by the Portuguese poet and cultural attaché at the Portuguese embassy in Paris, Luís Chaves de Oliveira (known also as Luís de Macedo).

> Magnificent voice, captivating, admirably controlled, a voice with deep resonances, voice of ancestral nostalgia, voice of intelligent sensitivity, voice of sorrowful fados … Daughter of a race with a prestigious past, under her clasped hands all the nostalgia for adventure, all of the murmur of the sea, all the dreams of the [colonial] discoveries, [these] sing, they cry, and they are released in the poignant melancholy of the "fados."

Amália gave new nobility to "fado," a song of uncertain origin but which is the spiritual refuge . . . of the Portuguese soul . . . . Amália at the Olympia sang only "fados." Amália sings Lisbon, it is then the whole living capital, with its alleys and its people who smile in the sun, it is (these are her own words) "my big city of my small country." Amália sings the dramas of fishing villages, we then see Nazaré or any other beach in Portugal; and the sea, which in Portuguese is a masculine word, is an implacable and worthy adversary of men. Amália sings the national songs: she carries them around the world. The whole world has heard it, and the cheering applause comes from all corners of the earth.

His back jacket endorsement frames both Amália and fado for an international audience as his rhetoric amplifies her stardom. Portugal, and Amália's voice and persona, are rendered in terms that align with official state dictatorship-era representations and ideologies of fado and of Portugal from the 1950s (Portugal as ancient, nostalgia filled, linked to the colonial "discoveries"). His words also align with increased emphasis on shaping Portugal as a destination for international tourism, and fado tourism, during the 1950s and 1960s. Oliveira's words on the back of the album sleeve represent fado as the "soul of Portugal" and Amália Rodrigues as the voice of that soul, carrying the genre of the nation of Portugal to the ears of the world.

## "almost no one understood the meaning of the words"

I found no lyrics or translations in the Olympia program. The printed Olympia program includes references to just two of the songs she sings, "Barco Negro" (reminding audience members that they may have heard it in a recent film in which Amália appeared and on a popular record that has been making its way around France) and "Coimbra" (glossing the Portuguese university city, and the Portuguese, in romantic terms). Three versions of the albums that I have collected—the French, the British, and the Dutch—do not include lyrics in Portuguese or full translations either. The first two contain summary excerpts of song lyrics in translation; the Dutch version contains no summaries, only track listings. (The Japanese version on EMI/Odeon from the mid-1970s contains an insert with lyrics in both Portuguese and in Japanese translation.)[3] Many listeners of her Olympia album would not have understood Portuguese, just as many audience members at her first Olympia performances did not.

On the album, Amália's spoken interactions with the audience are sparse. She announces the name of the song in Portuguese, providing no translation or explanation. This approach differs from that in some of her later live albums, for example, the extraordinary live album from Tokyo's Sankei Hall from September 2, 1970 where she gives short explanations for some of the songs in English prior to singing them (extraordinary for the palpable charge heard between Amália and her audience, extraordinary also for her musical risk taking and breathtaking virtuosity and mastery).[4] This approach also differs from the way fado is currently exported on the international stage in live performance, where explanation to the audience or some form of spoken cultural translation, is the norm.

What might stand out then in listening when one doesn't understand the words, or perhaps understands just a gist of the words? What, then, is intelligible or legible? Do the sound and timbre of the singing voice, musical and physical gestures, become more prominent in one's attention? Even if listeners did not understand the words being sung, they likely had (and have) a framework to understand the basic forms of musical expectation (a grammar of expectation), of longing, and of arrival built into conventions of diatonic harmony and melody, upon which much popular song in the so called "West" is built. Fado is built on a diatonic system. This holds true even though Amália, in ornamenting with her voice, deftly moves through pitches, sliding between them sometimes, singing in the spaces between the half-steps (approximating microtones).

Without knowing the language, then, this is a listening experience that for some of her audience would be perhaps at once familiar and strange (exotic). Familiar for many listeners would be the harmonic and melodic expectations of the diatonic system. Familiar also, might be some of the cross-cultural crying icons I mentioned earlier. Exotic (or even strange perhaps), might be the particular ways in which she ornaments with her voice, the sonority of the language in which sings, the ways in which she plays with meter and draws out notes, the juxtaposition between moments where she is aligned with the harmonic framework provided by the instrumentalists and the moments where she momentarily escapes from this in a drawn-out slide between two notes, or a scooping up into a note, or a little turn of the voice.

# the "otherness" of Amália's sound and style

Initially, some Portuguese critics objected to what they heard as a "Spanish" style to Amália's style of melismatic vocal ornamentation. Amália, aligning herself with both the rural and the national, claimed that her mother's vocal style had influenced her, and more specifically, vernacular styles of everyday singing (not fado) from the Beira Baixa region of Portugal (her mother's birthplace) had influenced her manner of vocal ornamentation (Santos 2005 [1987], 60). Just as her voice would be cast in national terms from within Portugal (her voice as the "soul" of the nation), the dictatorial regime also celebrated the rural, the agrarian, and the folk in contrast to the decadence of the city (Melo 2001). Amália, in locating the roots of her vocal style in Portuguese rurality, calls to mind a similar move that the ethnomusicologist Virginia Danielson (1997) has noted regarding the vocal style and career of the twentieth-century Egyptian diva Umm Kulthum, in which she strategically appealed to both her rural roots and to an urban audience, shaping her national appeal as the "voice of Egypt." In appealing to the influence of the singing styles of her mother from the Beira Baixa, Amália, who lived in Lisbon and had the most cosmopolitan and well-traveled career of any musician during the regime, marks her voice as one of the rural, and of the urban, and also of "the people" (*povo*).

As her career became increasingly international in the 1950s, foreign critics would also grasp at ways to describe and place what they heard as her "special" or unique form of vocal styling and her sound and its affective capacity. Critics often framed her voice in ways that exotified it or marked it as strikingly other. Following her Olympia debut, a critic for the French press, notes that [her voice] is "as plaintive as an injured animal," othering the sound and expressive power of her sound by comparison to the animal or non-human.[5] Of her 1952 performance at New York's club La Vie en Rose, in which she performed both fado and Spanish song, the critic in *The New*

*Yorker* column "Tables for Two" concludes his review by attempting to describe what he hears technically in her voice, grasping for analogies:

> Apart from the special appeal of the songs themselves, there is a fascination in just following the swift, easy succession of her tones, for she often divides a single note into two or three parts by sudden alterations in volume and timbre, without any slackening of tempo. It's a trick, but a delightful one. In many ways, her style is similar to Hebrew chanting, with its bewildering convolutions, but her singing is much gentler and not bewildering. Maybe a muted version of a muezzin's call to prayer is what I'm thinking of. Anyway, it is something special.
>
> October 25, 1952, 136

This critic, attempting to explain what he hears as "special" in her voice, compares her vocal style and technique to "Hebrew chanting," which he characterizes as replete with "bewildering convolutions" (an unfortunate choice of words which marks Hebrew chanting as unintelligible) and as a "muted version of a muezzin's call to prayer." Situating her voice as not quite "Jewish" and not quite "Arab," (a voice of religious Islam in prayer), he frames her voice as *outside* and as *other* to stylistic norms with which he is familiar (and in so doing also as other to the dominant Christian religious majority in the United States at the time). The othering of her voice by this critic, by means of description of her melismas (her so called "bewildering convolutions" in which she sings multiple pitches on one syllable), is in line with a long practice in the United States and Western Europe of the othering of vocalities of the "foreign," the "folk," or minorities. In this context, the melisma has sometimes served as a particularly charged mark of otherness (Meizel 2011, 267–272).

# gendering and mystifying her voice and presence

Exotifying descriptions of her vocal style and sound for foreign export, during the 1950s sometimes went hand-in-hand with gendered descriptions of her appearance and stereotypes about femininity (noting her "beauty," often calling attention to her mouth, her lips, her face, or her hair in sensual terms) and with statements about the affective power of her voice. This same critic at *The New Yorker* introduced his readers to Amália as, "a short, vibrantly healthy young thing, with a square face, framed in a wealth of black hair, and big, lustrous eyes." The page in the program that introduces Amália to the Olympia public in 1956, describes her as "the beautiful Amalia" (*belle*). The critic, Paul Carrière of *Le Figaro*, in an excerpted review from April 18, 1956, included on the back of the French release of the Olympia album, notes:

> Portuguese singer Amalia Rodrigues gave us an extraordinary moment. With a sovereign beauty, she stands far from the microphone, almost motionless, limiting herself to playing her fingers in the fringes of her shawl. But her deep eyes, her lips, and her whole face manifest a life of such intensity of feelings that one is held captive and does not ask for more.

Jean Teixcier, of the literary magazine *La Nouvelle Revue* (NRF) (November 1956 issue), in an excerpt on the back of the French release of the Olympia album, notes that "motionless, she sings in the language of her country" and that he is grateful that she didn't sing in French. He describes the "notes and words from her homeland," that she sings, as seemingly not "exactly formed by her lips or mouth" but rather "they [her notes and words] emerge, in a hot and raspy pain as if shaped by her 'oppressed throat'." This reads as if the body of Amália is being almost acted *upon* ("her oppressed [or afflicted] throat" [*gorge oppressée*]) rather than emphasizing that the affective power of her vocal expression is linked to her artistic and technical mastery. *Does the fact that Amália sings in a language that the critic does not understand make this kind interpretation, of gendered and sexualized objectification, more facile for the critic?*

Amália's voice and persona were often presented as "mysterious."[6] Oliveira's endorsement on the back of the album comments on her performance style and singing: "Standing erect, dark from head to toe, without gesturing, shoulders wrapped in a large shawl, face turned toward an interior dream, eyes half-closed, figurehead of an ancient caravel, she sings. She sings as one prays, with a penetrating and mystical grandeur, allowing her entire soul to be divined." The fact that so much of Amália's Olympia public and so many consumers of the live album did not understand Portuguese, may have worked to shift the focus of these listeners even more toward the *sound* of her voice and the *feeling* transmitted by that sound. For audience members at her live Olympia performances, that lack of linguistic knowledge could have also served to heighten their attention to the visual. The lack of linguistic understanding cloaks her voice in mystery, heightening an aura of mystery upon which listeners can then inscribe their own personal narratives or perhaps enter more readily into a "transcendental" experience.[7]

While some of her critics during the 1950s wrote about her in ways that clearly exotified her stage presence, her sound, and vocal expression in gendered terms, at least one critic notes that the presentation of femininity that Amália displayed in these first Olympia performances was atypical. Roger Féral, one of France's most important men in the media and culture industry at the time, and the director of the live television program *Télé-Paris* (Caille 2009, 74), wrote a review for the publication *France-Soir* (from April 20, 1956), excerpted on the back of the album jacket, describing her debut:

> In front of a curtain, a singer still unknown in Paris had arrived, without stage setting, without a plunging neckline [*sans décolleté*], with nothing but two guitarists, a black dress and shawl and her talent: Amalia Rodrigues. She sang seven songs in Portuguese. Almost no one understood the meaning [of the words], but the miracle happened, the same miracle that once made Raquel Meller a world star overnight. The public, from the orchestra [front/stalls] to the flies [*aux cintres*], was taken, conquered, subjugated, carried away.

That Féral noted that she accomplished "this miracle" "sans décolleté," that she conquered the audience without showing cleavage, marks a sexualized female stage presentation as the norm and Amália as departing from this norm.

I remember the small metal weight on the inside of the neckline of her stage dresses, there to ensure her modesty, likely at least partially related to cultural values surrounding Portuguese female modesty at the time (see Chapter 1).

Amália, in her Olympia performances, is not only exporting the Portugal of sun, of sea, of colonial nostalgia for touristic consumption on the international stage, she is also exporting a particular representation of 1950s Portuguese femininity and womanhood.[8]

# Interlude I: Mid-Century Representations: "Introducing Portugal"

*(1955, The Atlantic Community Series: NATO film 17m58s)*

Portugal joined NATO in 1949, included in the alliance even though António de Oliveira Salazar's *Estado Novo* (New State) regime was a dictatorship. From the perspective of the U.S. and NATO, two possible motivations for Portuguese inclusion: (1) Portugal's Azores islands are in a strategic location, halfway between the United States and Europe (and Allied forces had already made use of a base in the Azores during World War II, although Portugal officially began the war as "neutral");[1] (2) through legitimizing and aiding the *Estado Novo*, NATO inclusion might help to suppress communism in Portugal. "Antipathy to communism" was something also shared by the Portuguese regime and helped to fuel Portugal's political cold-war engagement with the USA (Rollo 2011, 6). In 1974 when a bloodless coup led by the Portuguese military toppled the regime, communist organizing would play a key role. The city of Lisbon would host a critical meeting for the restructuring of the alliance in 1952 (and in 1955, Portugal joined the United Nations). "Introducing Portugal" is one of several mini-documentaries on individual countries in the alliance produced as part of NATO's information campaign to introduce member states to one another.

Brass and the crashing of symbols. Flags of NATO member states wave in the wind. Images of craggy Portuguese coastline with crashing waves, lilting violins and the sounds of waves on the soundtrack: the suave voice of narrator, the Canadian actor Robert Beatty, begins as if telling a tale to children, "Portugal, 400 miles of ocean breakers, last barrier to the grey waters of the Atlantic, rolling in to die amid the flying surf." … The sound of brass: "A favorite excursion for Lisbon schoolchildren is to the city's famed Maritime Museum, shrine of the great age of Portuguese exploration." "The Portuguese set out in 50-tonne caravels to push back the frontiers of the unknown with their skillful exploration." Arrows appear on a map with lines drawing Portuguese sea routes and "discoveries." As Beatty lists them, dates appear on the screen: "The Azores in 1423; Cape Bojador in 1433; West Africa crossing the equator in 1473; after the Congo the Cape of Good Hope was reached in 1488 opening the way to East Africa, and in 1498 the sea route to India and the Far East." We see "rugged faces" "which bear witness to the strong individual character of this land and its people." Portugal, we learn, is "now selling abroad almost twice as much as before the war" and "she passes on not only her own products, but also those of her great dependent territories, like Angola and Mozambique."[2]

In just under eighteen minutes, the film covers extraordinary ground, juxtaposing images and narratives of "modern" and "traditional" Portugal, military capability, political alliances (historic and contemporary), emphasizing its attractiveness as a tourist destination, and legitimizing the Portuguese dictatorship and its colonial project, and representing Portugal as a stable democracy with free elections. We hear of "new dams and hydroelectric schemes," see "gleaming gas stations and smart hotels," and modern bridges and roads. There is a bullfighter in a sequined costume with a bull in the ring, men herding livestock to the sounds of folkloric singing, men on boats with billowing white sails on the Douro River, transporting barrels of Port wine. Then there are the constant references to military prowess, sometimes including a musical leitmotiv with ascending brass and the crashing of cymbals: histories of "armies marching and counter marching," the Portuguese naval fleet. Portuguese squadrons, "equipped with NATO jets" turn pirouettes in formation in the sky over the Atlantic. Men line up to cast their vote in the ballot box as the narrator announces "… the man in the street makes the best use of his vote, for he knows only too well the value of stable government. This spirit can be seen in the respect shown the man who in 1928 began to steer his country towards its present stable economy, Prime Minister Salazar" (sounds of applause).

A little over halfway through, an unseen *guitarra* faintly sounds. The volume rises, and the voice of Amália enters singing an ebullient song about Lisbon in the genre of a march (*marcha*). In the lyrics, a "little old lady" born "eight centuries ago" (referring to Lisbon) tells how Lisbon is a beautiful girl and will always remain a girl (*menina*). The lyrics begin: "All of the city floats / In the sea of my song / They pass on the street / Pieces of the moon / That fall from my balloon."[3] To a soundtrack of Amália singing, images of city life appear on the screen, contrasting the old and new: women in the neighborhood of Alfama carrying bundles atop their heads, men in suits walking to work on a busy street. The narrator informs us that the population of the city has doubled in size in just fifty years and the camera pans to the "Lisbon of today and tomorrow" (high-rise buildings, new wide boulevards).

Amália's voice cuts out then returns in a scene showcasing Portugal's temperate climate and leisure activities: horses race on a track, a man swings a golf club, people swim and sail. Her voice fades out but returns at the end as the credits roll, singing the same song. She is never seen, only heard, and her name does not appear in the credits.

# PART 2

# Listening to *Amalia à l'Olympia*

# Prelude: On Love and Longing

*There are so many ways to listen to this album. Even though this is not a concept album (an album intentionally created around one central idea or concept), what might we learn by listening to it as a whole, putting the tracks in conversation with one another? Every song on this album opens up into so many stories and histories. There are stories of composition and reception and of the shapeshifting of musical sounds and styles. There are histories of networks, places, nations, and politics, and of genre, artistry, poets, and musicians. There are gendered histories, raced histories. And then there is the question of love, the subject of longing (*saudade*). There are so many love songs on this album. How might we understand these excessive labors of love and longing?*

The song lyrics (poems) on Amália's 1957 Olympia album, and the curated stories they tell, taken together, teach listeners how to understand Amália's voice, as a Portuguese voice, as a woman's voice, a crying voice, as the voice of fado. They sing a sadness that is almost always bittersweet (as in the tracks "Barco Negro" [Black Boat], "Lisboa Antiga" [Old Lisbon], "Ai Mouraria") or where one transcends ill fate by being strong ("Sabe-se Lá" [Who Might Know]). They report on a beautiful, soulful and nostalgic Lisbon and Portugal where sometimes even poverty is a joyful virtue ("Lisboa Antiga," "Ai, Mouraria," "Uma Casa Portuguesa" [A Portuguese House]).

Many of the song lyrics on the album also teach listeners particular ideas about what the genre of fado is. As in the genre of the blues, fado also has a tradition of lyrics that self-reflexively comment back on the genre itself (Chapters 3 and 8). In these fados about fado, lyrics might reference its instruments, affects, its histories, its lore, its venues, city and neighborhoods, fadistas and instrumentalists of the past and its characteristic sounds and timbres ("Tudo Isto É Fado" [All of This is Fado], "A Tendinha" [The Little Tavern], "Que Deus Me Perdoe" [May God Forgive Me (for loving fado)]. Many of the album's lyrics convey certain ideas of femininity and masculinity, and most of all, dwell in conceits of romantic heterosexual love, in seduction, in loss, in longing, in flirtation, in pursuit, and in the maintenance of feminine honor ("Perseguição" [Pursuit], "Ai Mouraria," "Nem às Paredes Confesso" [Not Even to the Walls Would I Confess], "Amália" [a fado song with her name as title]). Just as Maurice Carrère framed fado as a love song, in his Olympia program endorsement, even though this statement doesn't accurately reflect the nuanced history of the genre, "Fado is a love song, almost always melancholy and often heartbreaking," most of the songs on this album are in some way about romantic (heterosexual) love.[1]

This emphasis on romantic love in the songs of this album reflects a wider shift in fado lyrics under the censorship in Portugal during this era, reflecting both fado's increasing use as a "national song" in the final decades of the Salazar regime and the promotion of fado in relation to tourism. The increasing turn to "love" and melancholy in fado lyrics of this era counters fado's previous histories in relation to social protest (Costa and Guerreiro 1984 and Nery 2004 as cited in Gray 2013, 96–97). During this time, the Portuguese regime had an active political police, the politically outspoken could be taken prisoner, and fado lyrics were subject to censorship. In the postwar moment, fado becomes more audible on the international stage through the voice of Amália and fado's "love" partakes in the Hollywood currency of romantic love (Berlant 2008). Love, as both particular and "universal," particularly when combined with nostalgia (or saudade in this case), is a powerful mix and can function as a smokescreen for political realities and lived experiences of struggle (Gray 2013, 192, 290).

# **5** Presentation and "Uma Casa Portuguesa" (A Portuguese House)

Track 1: side A

> "Une maison portugaise"
>
> In a Portuguese home there is always bread and wine on the table and however humble the person who knocks on the door, he will be invited to share what we have. The richness of poverty is to know how to give with joy, and the people are always faithful to this. Four whitewashed walls, with Saint Joseph above the entrance, a few bunches of grapes, two roses in the small garden, a sun in an eternal spring, two waiting arms with a promise of kisses … Ah, it's a Portuguese home!
>
> *translation of the French lyrics summary on the back jacket*

Listen. You hear the voice of a woman, fast speaking, in French, almost breathless, the presenter. She announces the instrumentalists and then introduces Amália Rodrigues as the "great Portuguese star," drawing out the final "a" in "Amália" with a flourish. The instrumentalists strike a chord and the audience applauds simultaneously immediately after she finishes saying "Rodrigues!" Through this applause Amália speaks a quiet "obrigada" (thank you) and then in French, "merci bien." A steel string brilliant strummed chord from Domingos Camarinha, on the Portuguese guitar (*guitarra*), sets the key for the song; this helps the fadista get the key in her inner ear before singing. "Casa Portuguesa," announces Amália. You hear the guitarra figuring an upbeat melody and the steady bass notes of the *viola* (Spanish acoustic guitar) underneath. Amália enters singing.

"Uma Casa Portuguesa" is a cheerful song in duple meter (I have seen sheet music versions notated in both 2/2 and in 2/4 time). The lyrics begin by presenting characteristics of an ideal Portuguese home, one in which it is good to have bread and wine on the table, to welcome visitors to share what one has (even if one doesn't have much). They present poverty as happiness and a scenario where humble hospitality and generosity constitute their own rewards. The refrain describes visual, sensual and affective qualities of this idealized Portuguese house, its whitewashed walls, the hint of a scent (*cheirinho*) of rosemary in the air, a bunch of golden grapes hanging, two roses in the garden, a traditional Portuguese ceramic tile (*azulejo*) depicting Saint Joseph, the sun of springtime, the promise of kisses, two arms waiting to embrace. The refrain, in melody and words, is so catchy that it could be a jingle, its catchiness heightened with the repeated rhyming three syllable words of *portuguesa* and *certeza*, in the phrase at the end (It is a Portuguese house, for certain / For certain it is a Portuguese house).

The second verse begins, "In the poor (*pobrezinho*) comfort of my home / There is an abundance of affection (*carinho*) and concludes by noting that very little (*basta pouco pocochinho*) is needed to bring joy to such a simple life, just love, bread, and wine, and the traditional Portuguese kale and potato soup (*caldo verde*) simmering on the stove (the word green ["verde"] emphasized with "verdinho") ("caldo verde verdinho"). The lyrics for the song as a whole include numerous words with diminutive suffixes (-inho) which have the effect, in this context, of emphasizing smallness, and smallness of scale, and intimacy or affection. "Pobrezinho," which literally translates as "just a little bit poor" works to diminish the intensity of "pobre" (poor), imbuing it with affection; with "pouco poucochinho" even smallness ("pouco") is further diminished (to very very little). To the listener who understands Portuguese, the lyrics could signal that this is a Catholic home (Saint Joseph), a home that in its poor simplicity is full of abundance. They signal the presence of the rural in the home, with the rosemary and the bunch of grapes, even if this home is in the city, and they signal to virtues of humility, hospitality, domesticity, generosity, loving affection, and of a humble acceptance of one's lot in life.

Listen to how Amália sings these lines from the refrain both times it comes around (1:18–1:26 and 2:24–2:33), "Uma promessa de beijos / Dois braços à minha espera" (A promise of kisses / Two arms waiting for me). Listen to how right before the phrase begins, the instrumentalists slightly slow down the tempo to give more prominence to the line to come, heightening the drama of her voice by focusing the attention on it. The *guitarra* and *viola* then create a momentary silence, pausing as she sings into that space, showcasing a luxurious slide in her voice as she scoops upwards on the vowel "u" of *uma* into the consonant "m." Instrumentalists and fadista have now both slowed the pace considerably and both Amália and her instrumentalists stretch out the meter in this phrase. Listen to the small ornamental lilt in her voice on the "e" in "promessa" (promise) and then note the way she draws attention to the word "beijos" (kisses) as she slides downwards from the "b" in "beijos" emphasizing the "ei" sound, so that the two-syllable word sounds almost like it has three. The way in which Amália and her instrumentalists play with meter, literally "stealing time," with their use of *rubati* in this section, heightens the emotive force of these lines, focused on a relation of love and physical affection, and also musically accentuates the phrases to come. Listen to how she holds the "a" at the end of "espera" (waiting) at the end of the phrase, the "a" sound remaining suspended for a moment before the instrumentalists pick up again in a faster tempo to lead into the last lines of the refrain, now back in a sing-song march.

On the surface, the lyrics may seem simple and happy. But for some Portuguese listeners, this is a weighty and charged song. I try to listen to her "Casa Portuguesa" here with new ears, with ears that haven't heard this song performed hundreds of times, in so many contexts by so many, and most of all with ears that haven't heard so many stories that gesture to the heavy political weight that the song, now over seventy years, since its composition, has accrued and that has so thoroughly saturated the Portuguese cultural sphere, at home and in diaspora. I try to listen without the knowledge that I have about how even the name of the song for some Portuguese has come to stand in for an entire propaganda complex during the *Estado Novo* regime.

When I listen anew, when I focus on Amália's artistry and her sound and the force of her music making, I hear a precision, an agility and fluidity in her voice and crystal-clear diction. There is a freshness in the sound of her voice and the song in her rendering. Her voice at the end of phrases at times floats with a lightly quivering vibrato, suspended in the air (as in the words "bem" [well/good] and "alguém" [someone] in the first verse). There is the expressivity through which she bends the meter, in the moment above that I describe in the refrain where she lingers in a luxurious expansiveness, employing her trademark rubati, injecting into the relentless cheerfulness and predictable march meter of the song, a hint of pathos.

Yet I cannot in my listening so easily erase meanings that the lyrics and melody have accrued over time. "The Portuguese house" can be read or heard as highly condensing multiple values of regime-era Portugal (Matos 2008, 111–112). There are so many potent regime-era ideologies working in tandem here through the use of symbols. Some of the values that these symbols gesture toward include: agrarianism or the rural (versus industrial modernity), the Catholic faith, the nuclear family, hospitality, humility, and the traditional place of women as keepers of the home (of the domestic sphere) and as progenitors of the nation (Matos 2008, 111–112). The abundance of diminutives and an idea of coziness they help to convey is in line with a cultural aspect of dictatorship-era Portugal in which miniaturization plays an important role in shaping and powerfully distilling metaphors of the nation (Gil 2007, Melo 2001, 7), and in this case, symbolically renders the Portuguese house as both a synecdoche (where the part stands in for the whole) and a microcosm of the nation. Because the values are fused and sonorously carried in song, they potentially have a greater sticking power (an earworm that gets *stuck* in the head) and additionally greater capacity to circulate, be remembered, and to move a listening public.

A drawing of a small rural home is etched on the cover of sheet music for "Uma Casa Portuguesa" (1953) that I find in Portugal's National Library.[1] The caption under the drawing (in Portuguese) reads "from the book *Casas Portuguesas* by Raul Lino." Raul Lino, a widely published and prominent twentieth-century Portuguese architect (see Lino 1998 [1944]) played a defining role in the "controversial Portuguese House Campaign," which linked architectural elements of the home to a specific Portuguese lifestyle (Pereira 2020, 2). Beneath the drawing of the house is a photograph of Amália on the right and a smaller photo of the singer Carlos Fernando on the left (under both photos, the words, "gravou em discos" [recorded on discs] with the names of their labels, "His Master's Voice" and "Columbia").

The lyrics were composed by the Portuguese poets Reinaldo Ferreira and Vasco de Matos Sequeira, likely in the Hotel Girassol in the port city of Lourenço Marques (now Maputo) in the former Portuguese colony of Mozambique.[2] In the mid-twentieth century, Lourenço Marques was a key nexus for South African trade, a popular international beach resort destination, and a thriving site of settler colonialism, with many white Portuguese "settlers" (Munslow 2005). The city's center "was reserved for whites only."[3] The song was likely first sung by the Portuguese-Angolan singer Sara Chaves, an announcer for Radio Angola and heard on Radio Mozambique in the early 1950s (Santos 2014, 493). Numerous Brazil-based ensembles and singers covered the song in the early 1950s, such as Olivinha Carvalho, Gilda Valença and Trio Madrigal.[4] Amália recorded it as early as 1953 and included it on her first album released in the United States on Angel Records in 1954. "Uma Casa Portuguesa" has since been recorded and/or performed on stage in diverse versions, including those by: the psychedelic rock group Os Morgans (Portugal), the Cape Verdean singer Johnny Rodrigues (Netherlands), the Portuguese-Brazilian singer Roberto Leal (Portugal), The Hazy Osterwald Sextet (Switzerland), and by the Brazilian singer João Gilberto.

While the ethos of the lyrics undeniably fits with regime era ideologies and propaganda of the time, it is not clear if these meanings were intended by the poets as such. The Portuguese journalist, Nuno Pacheco, observes that the lyrics could have been intended ironically, that according to a contemporary, the two poets were thinking about writing some pornographic poetry when Artur Fonseca, a Portuguese violinist, composer and conductor (and composer of the music for the song), living in Lourenço Marques, admonished them to have some respect, chiming in with the objection, "you are in a Portuguese house!" (uma casa portuguesa). Reinaldo Ferreira replied that "uma casa portuguesa" could be a good song title, to which Fonseca replied "com certeza" (with certainty) (inadvertently composing what would become part of the refrain). At the same time, Pacheco concedes that this story isn't certain.[5]

The post-dictatorship reception of "Uma Casa Portuguesa," both in Portugal and its diaspora, can be understood as one of *both/and*, not necessarily of *either/or*. Strong opinions continue to be voiced on both sides: the song as regime propaganda versus the song as innocent. Vítor Pavão dos Santos, in his book *O Fado da Tua Voz: Amália e os Poetas* (The fado of your voice: Amália and the poets), marks the song as one of the "greatest successes (perhaps the greatest?) in the history of Portuguese music" and writes, "It amazes me: 'Uma Casa Portuguesa,' a beautiful poem, so poorly judged by the simpleton intelligentsia reigning in Portugal, that took it for something *salazarista* [connected to the regime of the dictator Salazar]." He understands the lyrics as following in a poetic tradition of the pastoral or the bucolic and citing the ancient Roman poet Virgil, asks if it would be fair to say that Virgil was *salazarista* (Santos 2014, 492–493).

Rui Vieira Nery discusses an ideology propagated by Salazar's regime, of the "poor but honorable" ("pobrezinho mas honrado") which was criticized by the democratic opposition (given the "underdevelopment and misery that characterized daily life for the majority of Portuguese people" [during this time]). Yet he asks, "Is it legitimate to give excessive force to the political ideology expressed in a popular *cançoneta* [little song] at once so ingenuous and so happy, in terms of its music and poetic formulation, that the public, since the start, welcomed with such affection, an affection that has not diminished?" "Perhaps," he suggests, "we can at last start to look at this happy song ... without the weight of a political prejudice—thank God—that no longer makes sense" (2009, 155).

Nuno Pacheco writes about the reception of a concert in 2017 in Buenos Aires of the contemporary fado singer Mísia. The concert was linked to the launch of her album in homage to Amália, *Para Amália* (For Amália) (2015) and there were a number of Portuguese immigrants in the audience.[6] Mísia refused to sing "Uma Casa Portuguesa" when asked by an audience member; Pacheco cites the Portuguese newspaper *Expresso* claiming that Mísia was now labeled "persona non grata" by the Portuguese community in Argentina. He quotes an excerpt of an interview in the Portuguese *Notícias Magazine* where Mísia explains to the audience the reasons behind her decision, "I don't sing it on the album or in concerts.... I don't identify with the theme of the song; I think it is an apology for poverty."[7]

The playwright, Elaine Ávila, in her play, *Fado: The Saddest Music in the World*, crafts a place of ambivalence for "Uma Casa Portuguesa." A Portuguese immigrant living in Canada, a woman named Rosida, lies weeping on the floor after she hears of Amália's death in 1999. Her daughter Luísa, a recent college graduate, decides she would like to learn how to sing fado and that they should make a once in a lifetime journey to Lisbon. In preparation, she learns the song "Uma Casa Portuguesa," a favorite of her mother, only to be met with anger by a Portuguese guitar player in Lisbon, her teacher, for having brought to him such a "fascist" song that extols the "joy of poverty" (Ávila 2021, 13–15).

Some Portuguese fado aficionados who I spoke in Lisbon during my research there during the first decade of the 2000s, referenced the song as something that was sung in fado clubs primarily for tourists, and might point to the song as an example of how repertoire of fadistas had changed in response to tourism (Gray 2013, 114). At the same time, in one of the amateur fado venues where I did long-term research, which was mostly attended by Portuguese locals, I often heard fadistas sing "Uma Casa Portuguesa" to audible audience enjoyment (for example, listeners boisterously smacking their lips making kissing sounds when a fado singer would leave a silence after drawing out the word "beijos" [kisses]), even when I knew that the audience contained older members that had firmly been anti-regime during the dictatorship.

Ávila's, Nery's and Santos' interpretations, the polemic around the fadista Mísia's 2017 refusal to sing the song, and various reactions to the song I witnessed amongst members of Lisbon's amateur fado community, point to the multiple meanings and charged symbolic positioning of the song in both contemporary Portugal and in diaspora. Amália's Olympia recording greatly amplified "Uma Casa Portuguesa" beyond Portuguese speaking musical networks, the regime-era stereotypical "Portuguese home" traveling the world in sound. A song carries its social histories of listening forward into the present.

# 6 "Perseguição" (Pursuit)

Track 4: side A

"Poursuite"

You are rich and elegant, but your flowers and kisses won't make me your mistress. I refuse them and always will. I am married, I love my husband.

*translated excerpt of the French lyrics*
*summary on the back jacket*

Listen to Amália's voice as she sings the first line, "Se de mim, nada consegues" (If you get nothing from me). There is an almost playful lilt to the way she styles her entrance. She seems to hum slightly before articulating the "s" in the first word and then ornaments the one-syllable word "mim" (me) with a descending three-note *voltinha*. The first verse continues, "I don't know why you pursue me / constantly in the street / you know that I am married and that I can never be yours." The poem "Perseguição" was written by Avelino de Sousa and its lyrical melody by Carlos da Maia. The tale it tells is about a married woman in love with her husband and dedicated to him but who is relentlessly pursued by a suitor. He is rich and elegant (and vain), and no match for the poor husband, who has a "noble soul."

Musically and poetically, "Perseguição" is an example of *fado tradicional* (traditional fado) because each verse repeats the same underlying melodies and harmonies and the number of poetic lines in a verse is fixed. (Another song on the album with a traditional fado structure is "Fado Corrido," track 6, side A.) In "Perseguição," each verse is comprised of six lines of poetry (*sextilhas*). Each verse has three separate rhymes falling on the final syllable of a line of the verse (rhyme pairings: the first and second lines, the third and sixth lines, and the fourth and fifth lines). In terms of performance, one of the characteristics of traditional fado form is that the fadista "styles" (or improvises) each verse slightly differently.

"Perseguição" was one of the very first fados Amália recorded, in a live recording from Rio de Janeiro in 1945; it would become a mainstay of her repertoire.[1] Avelino de Sousa wrote the lyrics for the fado singer Maria Alice (Santos 2014, 73), who recorded it on shellac in 1936 and who popularized the song in Brazil.[2] For much of fado's history, it was expected that fadistas would have their own unique poetic repertoire; for this reason, the fact that Amália chose to record "Perseguição" as one her first fados stands out. By the time Amália sang "Perseguição" at the Olympia in 1956, it had already been twice made a hit, first by Maria Alice and then through the voice of Amália, who transformed it both stylistically and lyrically. Amália's "Perseguição" is the one that has had staying power.

While this traditional fado commonly bears the name of the very first lyrics that accompanied the melodic base for "Perseguição," as a traditional fado form, it has also been subsequently sung and recorded with many different poems. One contemporary example that stands out is the Portuguese fadista António Zambujo's 2010 recording with the lyrics "Apelo."[3] But even when a singer uses completely different lyrics, many fado instrumentalists and singers, still name the musical base of this fado "Perseguição" (after the lyrics to which it was most famously sung).

Listen to the 1936 recording by Maria Alice and compare it to Amália's Olympia recording.[4] You might notice how where Amália languorously stretches the meter, Maria Alice hews closer to its confines and sings it straighter, with far less vocal ornamentation (although she does stretch out the meter at some of the line ends, for added emphasis). You may also notice that the two fadistas sing different final verses to the poem. Vítor Pavão dos Santos recounts how in 1943, Amália was singing in Madrid and the Portuguese ambassador to Spain, Pedro Teotónio Pereira, requested that she sing "Perseguição," which Maria Alice had made a hit.[5] Amália refused, finding the original final verse, in which the protagonist declares herself a "vigilant sentinel" protecting her husband's honor, in "bad taste." Pereira wrote a substitute final verse for Amália (Santos 2014, 73) which begins, "I tore up your letters without reading them" and continues, "and never wanted to receive the jewelry or flowers that you sent." When the actor and fado singer Ester de Abreu recorded it in 1952, in a version with orchestra on the Brazilian label Sinter, she included the verse substituted by Amália.[6]

It is this substitute final verse that Amália sings on the Olympia album. The verse possibly gives the female protagonist of the song a bit more agency than the first version and also adds more drama. Listen to the final verse on the Olympia album (1:36), starting with "Rasguei as cartas sem ler" (I tore up your letters without reading them). She sings the full verse, but then she is silent; the guitarra takes over the vocal line and "sings" it for her, repeating the first three lines of the melody. Amália enters halfway through the final verse, repeating the last three lines for added emphasis, "I will not sell myself or give myself to you / Because I have already given everything that I am / To a love which you don't know." Regardless of choice of final verse, the lyrics tell a story of a woman devoted to her man, of heterosexual romantic love and marriage. The moral the lyrics drive home is about the duty of the wife to stay faithful and preserve her husband's honor at all costs.

# 7 "Barco Negro" (Black Boat)

Track 7: side A

(Printed on the disc: "Barco Negro, du filme 'Les Amants du Tage' [Caco Velho – Piratini et D. J. Ferreira]")

"Bateau noir"

This is the anguished cry (*cri d'angoisse*) of a woman who refuses to believe in the death of her lover, a fisherman who has disappeared into the sea. She clearly sees a black cross on a rock; that frightens her (*qui lui fait peur*). The old women on the beach say that he will never return. They are crazy, crazy (*folles, folles*).

*translation from lyrics summary in French on back jacket*

Applause. Amália, speaking over the applause, announces "Barco Negro," followed by a "merci" with a smile in her voice. A silence. Listen to Amália's Olympia rendition of "Barco Negro." The guitarra and viola enter in 2/4 time, marking a steady repeated rhythm of dotted eighth note and sixteenth note, followed by two eighth notes, introducing the melody from the refrain. Just as they are getting started, the audience applauds again. Amália enters, in lock step with her instrumentalists, beginning the first verse which starts, *De manhã, que medo* … (In the morning, I awake, trembling on the sand, afraid that you will think I am ugly.)

The lyrics, composed by the Portuguese poet David Mourão-Ferreira, are dramatic; they tell a story of a woman waiting for her seafaring lover. Even though the word *saudade*, that quintessentially Portuguese form of nostalgic longing, never appears in the lyrics, the story is saturated with saudade, an unfulfilled longing for what was, what might be. The story also resonates with maritime narratives in relation to Portuguese nationalism (and colonialism), narratives of diaspora, and of Portuguese women waiting for their seafaring lovers to return (Gray 2013, 70–71,165; Silva 2019, 216). The music is dramatic too. There are the leaps in register, the driving percussive rhythm of the refrain, sudden shifts from major to minor. Amália masterfully exploits this surplus of drama with her soulful downward slides between pitches, with her *voltinhas*, with her drawn out melismas, with shifts and swells in volume and breath, her timbral nuances. She signals anguish partially through her use of icons of crying, particularly with her descending glissandi both large and small.

Listen to how she sings the word "olhos" (eyes), in the next phrase, crying in song with a downward slide through an interval of a fourth: "os teus olhos" … (your eyes) and listen to the shorter descending glissando that follows on the word "não" (no) in "disseram que não" (they told me that this was not true). Listen to the little vocal ornament (*voltinha*) she sings on the word *meu* (my) on "E o sol penetrou no meu coração" (And the sun penetrated my heart) in the following phrase. Listen to how she repeats the glissando and the ornament just a little bit differently when she sings these lines again.

"Vi depois," (I later saw), she sings … "a cross on a rock and your black boat dancing in the light … the old women on the beach said that you would not return." Listen to how this section sounds somewhat like sung speech, while the phrase moves gradually upwards in pitch with many repeated notes, on pitches that are close together, many just one step apart. Listen then to her silence, the way in which her silence frames the sound of a steady hand tapping on the wood of the instrument. Amália bursts forth, "São loucas" (They are crazy) (1:38–1:43) and then she repeats the words (1:46–1:50). The first "loucas," outlines a musical interval of a perfect fourth, upwards on the first syllable, and then back down with a weeping slide between pitches. Again her silence, more rhythmic tapping. In the second "são loucas," she dramatically shifts register, dropping down a full octave, then ascending an interval of a dark minor sixth, then sliding down a minor third. (Of her "são loucas," Amália once said, "When I gave that scream, *São loucas, são loucas*, sometimes I shivered all over, almost arriving right in the tragedy" [Santos 2005 (1987), 119]). She begins the refrain, her voice almost chant-like: "Eu sei meu amor" (I know my love) "… that you have never left, everything around me tells me that you will always be with me."

She moves into the second verse (which has the same melody as the first) singing of all the ways her beloved will remain with her, in the wind that blows the sand up against the windowpanes, in the "dying embers of the fire," in the "water that sings," in her heart. Listen, then, to her melisma and descending slide in a moment of extended weeping in song (vocal icons of crying), first on the exclamation "ai" (2:53–3:05) and then repeated beginning with sound "mm" (3:09–3:12) before then returning to "ai" (3:12–3:21). She again chants the refrain, pausing after the word "sempre" (always), the instrumentalists play into the silence, then she sings, "comigo" (with me), sliding upwards into the second syllable, accentuating it, prolonging the note, lowering her volume, the vibrations of her voice, suspended, for just a moment, in the space of the hall. Applause.[1]

Many in the Olympia audience, and some of the consumers of the Olympia album, would have known this song from the cinema, from Amália's role in the film *Les Amants du Tage* and the international release of the soundtrack recording of the film that followed. Some would have remembered the scene where the two lead characters fall in love as Amália sings. In the pivotal scene, Amália's character (also named "Amália") enters descending into a packed fado club via a circular staircase. The room is filled to capacity, the light is dim, the tables are lit with candles, some people stand along a back wall. Everyone is applauding, all eyes turn toward Amália as she makes her way down the stairs. She is wearing a long-sleeved V-neck black dress which skims her ankles, and a black lace fringed shawl is draped around her shoulders. She pauses. People shout out, the applause intensifies. The instrumentalists begin their introduction to "Barco Negro," accompanied by the sound of a drum beating out the dotted eighth note rhythm, or a hand on the wood of a *viola* (the source of percussive sound is not seen). When she sings her first set of "São loucas," the camera moves in closer, focusing in on her face.

A Frenchman (Pierre: played by Daniel Gélin) and a young Frenchwoman (Kathleen: played by Françoise Arnoul), who are in Portugal fleeing the law and whose passionate affair is the main theme of the film, are there together at a table sitting amongst the audience of Portuguese and tourists. As Amália sings "Barco Negro," the emotional intimacy between the two lead characters is cemented through the alchemy of her singing voice which translates into tears in Kathleen's eyes. As Amália sings, Pierre translates the Portuguese words of the song to Kathleen in a hushed intensity, and as Amália repeats the phrase "São loucas" ("They are crazy") with descending glissandi, with that octave descent in register, Kathleen's eyes well up with tears.

Tiago Baptista points out that one of enduring effects of *Les Amants du Tage* was to set a visual precedent for the cinematic techniques and camera angles used to shoot and frame Amália. He shows how these techniques direct the viewer's attention in specific ways to her face and body while she is singing that contrast with the focus an audience member might have during a live performance, in which the attention would be primarily directed to the voice. Through strategic use of the close up, particularly in the scene where she sings the song "Barco Negro," she is rendered, in filmic conventions, a star (Baptista 2009, 66–74). Close ups occur at moments of maximum emotional intensity of the song, first when Amália weeps on "São loucas" and then on the long drawn-out exclamation "ai," again those melismas and descending vocal slides, and then repeats on the sound "mm," her face filling the entire screen as she sings, the camera close up intensifying and focusing the expressivity of that moment sonorously and visually, directing ear and eye to pay heightened attention. This visual framing of Amália in the film primes Amália's international Olympia public in 1956 (and the consumers of the album that followed) to receive her in outsized dimensions, larger than life, a celebrity on the big screen and on the stage. It also links affects of crying and unfulfilled longing to a stereotypical idea of fado (intended for foreign consumption) and to her voice and image.

Returning to the album back jacket, the song summary itself does not directly translate the lyrics from Portuguese into French. Rather, it takes interpretive liberties, in some cases ascribing emotions to the protagonist of the song that are not signaled in the lyrics themselves (i.e., "the anguished cry," the black cross that "frightens her"). The words on the back jacket direct the French public how to listen to the album (and specific songs) in relation to particular emotional states and to link these to Amália's voice.

# Black Boat and/or Black Mother/Nanny: circulations, controversies, reverb

The acclaimed Black Brazilian samba musician and composer Mateus Nunes (known as Caco Velho) and the Brazilian songwriter Antônio Amábile (Piratini) composed the song "Mãe Preta" in the 1930s. The lyrics of "Barco Negro" were set to the music for "Mãe Preta." This history is commonly known by older Portuguese listeners, many of whom told me that the lyrics to "Mãe Preta" were censored by the dictatorial regime because they were about slavery, thus the new lyrics, "Barco Negro," were written by David Mourão-Ferreira. According to Amália, "The success [of "Barco Negro"] was so great that later, Caco Velho was playing in a [French] club named *Macumba* and he was selling a record of his that said "Caco Velho, composer of *Barco Negro*." She said also, "in the beginning, I didn't know that the music was Brazilian. I thought it was African" (Santos 2005 [1987], 119).

Caco Velho's group Conjunto Tocantins first recorded "Mãe Preta" in 1943.[2] "Mãe Preta" tells the story of a Black nanny, "rocking the cradle of her master's son" who "cheerfully raises every white child" while "later back in the slave quarters," "she wipes off one more tear." The words of the refrain, "Enquanto a chibata batia no seu amor / Mãe preta embalava o filho branco

**Figure 1:** *Cover art, sheet music for piano and voice, "Mãe Preta," Lisbon, Valentim de Carvalho, 1953 (permission granted), collection of the Biblioteca Nacional de Portugal*

do sinhô," translate as "while the cane whipped her love / Black nanny rocked her master's white son."

There is a black shaded rectangle, on the right side of the cover, of the sheet music arrangement for piano and voice of "Mãe Preta" that I find in Portugal's National Library in 2018

(Figure 1). There is a drawing of a Black woman with short white hair, wearing hoop earrings, holding a white baby in her arms. The skin of the white child glows incandescent against the stark black of the background, while the skin of the Black woman fades into the black. Underneath is the song title in stylized white capital letters. On the left are the words, "O maior sucesso da actualidade" (the biggest hit today), "O mais famoso batuque brasileiro" (The most famous Brazilian *batuque*), "de [of] Piratini and Caco Velho."The first copyright is listed as 1945 assigned by Editora Litero-musical TUPY S/A in São Paulo Brazil, for "all of the countries in the world" ("todos países do mundo") and the second copyright assigned in 1953 by Cembra, Lda., São Paulo and also by Valentim de Carvalho, Lisbon for continental Portugal and *ultramarino* [the Portuguese colonies]). A *batuque* was a dance of likely "Angolese or Congolese origin" but the term came to be understood in Brazil to refer to "Afro-Brazilian dance accompanied by heavy percussion" (Béhague 2001, 37). The use of "batuque" on this sheet music arrangement here is perhaps a gesture to indicate "in the style of" rather than to indicate the genre itself. "Mãe Preta" was covered by multiple artists in the 1950s.[3]

The Portuguese fadista Maria da Conceição recorded the song in 1954 with the original lyrics intact.[4] In 1954 Conceição's recording of Mãe Preta appeared on 78 rpm shellac discs produced by Odeon (Brazil), Discos Estoril (Portugal), and Iberia (Spain).[5] The scholars Guilhermina Lopes and Lenita Nogueira, hear a "fado" style and delivery in her 1954 recording (in her use of "chest voice, portamento, chromaticism, and a form of lamentation") and speculate that Amália may have had access to Maria da Conceição's recording, and that Caco Velho himself may have shared it with her. They note some similarities between her "Mãe Preta" and Amália's "Barco Negro" (Lopes and

Nogueira 2019, 42). Amália was likely familiar with Conceição's version (Santos 2005 [1987], 118).

Maria da Conceição's "Mãe Preta" and Amália's "Barco Negro," both played roles in the fado-fication of Caco Velho's "samba"/"batuque."[6] Even though it was Conceição's recording that possibly first made the melody known in Portugal, it is perhaps more likely that Maria da Conceição's vocal styling owes something to Amália's general stylistic influence on the genre of fado than it is that Amália's styling of the song was influenced by Maria da Conceição's recording. By 1954, Amália's voice and celebrity were already playing an outsized role, in Portuguese and Brazilian markets, for reshaping the stylistic possibilities for fado singing. Amália's voice, in her 1954 rendition of "Barco Negro" for the film *Les Amants du Tage* (which premiered in 1955), and in her 1956 Olympia recording, stands out for the ways in which the vocal affects of crying are heightened; her use of vocal slides, of portamenti, of glissandi, is more pronounced, more exaggerated, than in Conceição's "Mãe Preta."

Multiple narratives surrounding censorship in relation to "Mãe Preta" abound. The Brazilian journalist, Thaís Seganfredo, writes that Caco Velho claimed that the lyrics to "Mãe Preta" were censored in Portugal, but cites the researcher Rafa Rodrigues claiming that its original lyrics continued to be sung underground.[7] Lopes and Nogueira argue, that in a later 1958 recording by Maria da Conceição, the words "enquanto a chibata batia no seu amor" (while the cane beat her love) were censored in Portugal and substituted with "enquanto na senzala trabalhava o seu amor" (while her love worked in the slave quarters) (2019, 41). Some claim that censorship had nothing to do with the wholescale substitution of the lyrics of "Barco Negro" for "Mãe Preta." Amália claimed that those making

*Les Amants du Tage,* had "wanted lyrics that were less linked to specific circumstances and more beautiful, in keeping with the international distribution of the film" (Santos 2014, 667). Vítor Pavão dos Santos notes that there was "nothing political" in this decision to change the lyrics (2014, 667). The literary scholar, Daniel da Silva, cites David Ferreira, the son of the poet who wrote the lyrics for "Barco Negro," and longtime director of the Portuguese record company Valentim de Carvalho (later EMI Valentim de Carvalho, now EMI-Portugal), as noting that the argument that the lyrics were replaced due censorship is false, and that proof of this is that "the Angolan band Duo Ouro Negro recorded a version of 'Mãe Preta' in 1961 (Silva 2019, 216). Regardless, the narrative concerning the censorship of "Mãe Preta" in relation to the suppression of histories of slavery during the regime still circulates in Portuguese public culture around "Barco Negro" and remains an important part of the song's aura.

While "Barco Negro" is not a fado formally in any sense, the substitution of these lyrics in place of the original "Mãe Preta," first for the film *Les Amants du Tage*, and then in the Olympia album, followed a pattern well practiced with respect to traditional fado forms, in which singers or poets may set an infinite number of lyrics to any traditional musical structure as long as the lyrics meet specific poetic requirements in relation to the musical structure (for example, in terms of number of lines per stanza). This lyric substitution also follows the pattern I noted above, of shifting fado's sentiments more toward love and lament in the later years of the dictatorship under state censorship. As such, the theme of nostalgic romantic love in "Barco Negro" fits in with the Olympia album as a whole. Stylistically, the vocal crying icons that are present cross-culturally in multiple genres of lament and in stylized popular musics that draw on lament gestures, and are part and parcel of fado style, are exaggerated in Amália's "Barco Negro," potentially sympathetically or empathetically affecting even listeners who do not understand the words. I mentioned some of these moments at the beginning of this section: her downwards glissandi, on the words "são loucas"; her extended sung vocable (a vocal utterance without literal meaning) "ai,"; and her melismatic vocal ornamentation on key phrases.

In "Barco Negro" the lyrics of the original Brazilian "samba"/ "batuque" become purified, links to Portugal's histories of enslavement eradicated. This process is facilitated via the amplification platforms of the Olympia, the city of Paris—as the cosmopolitan center for musical consumption and sound recording—and through the voice of Amália Rodrigues, in her role as a musical ambassador for Portugal. The Brazilian "samba"/"batuque" is transformed into a fado, not only through the voice of the star fadista Amália, her virtuosity, and expressive force, but also through the alchemy of the French film industry and the platform of the Olympia.

The new lyrics are given heightened prestige when they circulate on Amália's Olympia album. The weeping of the Black nanny is supplanted by Portuguese seafaring "nationalist tropes" (Silva 2019, 16) and voiced in the Anglo/European genre of the weeping woman, one that scholar Lauren Berlant (2008) wrote about in relation to Hollywood and U.S. literary genres of "the female complaint" and which I have previously written about in relation to fado's, and Amália's feminine form of lament and stylized crying (Gray 2013).

"Barco Negro" shapeshifts yet again, in 1956, this time in French, in the flavor of a chanson with orchestral accompaniment, with the lyrics "Madona" by the contemporaneous Egyptian/French Olympia superstar vocalist

Dalida.[8] In the voice of Dalida, now in the song "Madona,""Barco Negro"/"Mãe Preta" is thus Europeanized, with French as the cosmopolitan European *lingua franca,* but Dalida mimics Amália's dramatic downward glissandi and vocal turns. These over-the-top moments of sung crying remain as sonic symbols of the exotic and the periphery (Portugal) as heard from Europe's postwar cultural center of Paris.[9] In 1958, the British conductor George Melachrino would record "Barco Negro" in a sweeping, instrumental-only, orchestral version for the LP *Lisbon at Twilight* (in which he failed to attribute Caco Velho and Piratini).[10]

"Barco Negro" became a mainstay of Amália's repertoire, which she recorded throughout her career in highly varied performances and remains one of the songs for which she is most internationally known. In international markets, the song sometimes stands in as iconic for the genre fado itself. "Barco Negro" has been a key part of the repertoire for some of the most internationally successful contemporary professional fadistas and remains a favorite for amateur and professional fado singers in Lisbon. When the young fadista Mariza broke onto the world music scene in the early 2000s, she covered "Barco Negro" on her debut album.[11] In 2021, she would include it on an Amália tribute album, and perform it in a concert "tour" for New York's Town Hall, live streamed from a recording studio in Lisbon, during a pandemic lockdown, her instrumentalists in black masks.[12] The fado singer Lina, one of the newest arrivals on fado's international scene, also included it on her 2020 debut album (on both compact disc and vinyl), produced by Raül Refree, in arrangement for voice, piano and vintage analog electronic sound effects.[13] (Refree had previously collaborated with the Spanish superstar vocalist Rosalía in 2017, on the debut album that launched her celebrity.)[14]

In multiple covers, retakes, and new lyric substitutions, some artists have turned the tables, critically reflecting back on the occluded original lyrics of "Mãe Preta" in their performances, histories of colonization and contact, or the voicing of protest. One such example is the Brazilian artist Ney Matogrosso's 1975 performance in his recording of "Mãe Preta (Barco Negro)." He does not only weep in stylized song as Amália does, but as Silva, who examines queer, indigenous and Afro-Brazilian intersections in Matogrosso's performance, points out, at the end, he actually cries (2019, 218). In this inconsolable weeping, Silva hears Matogrosso as "[making a] space for the black woman of this violent [colonial] history, for the loss and mourning put upon *mãe preta* to be heard" (224). Alternatively, Lopes and Nogueira hear in Matogrosso's break into sobs, a protest of Brazil's dictatorial regime (2019, 49).

Another example appears in the film, *O Sentido da Vida* (The Meaning of Life) (2021), in which the Portuguese filmmaker Miguel Gonçalves Mendes collaborates with the Japanese fado singer, Kumiko Tsumori following a young Brazilian man as he travels the world.[15] In a scene set in Japan, Tsumori sings "Barco Negro" in Japanese with a dual title ("The Wind That Cries") *O Vento Que Chora* (the Portuguese lyrics appear on the screen) as the soundtrack for a revisiting of narratives of Portuguese/Western encounter in Japan, with key moments narrated in script on the screen. We read of the first arrival of the Portuguese in 1543 in Tanegashima, and the introduction of firearms in Japan; the camera moves to the city of Nagasaki (the Portuguese made a base there in the mid-sixteenth century). Later in the clip, precisely at the moment in which Amália sings with the extended vocable "ai" in "Barco Negro," Kumiko Tsumori sings on the vowel sound "ah," and we see footage of the abandoned Nagasaki island city of Hashima, which Mitsubishi exploited for the extraction of coal, and which was declared a world heritage site by UNESCO in 2015. In suturing the cries of "Barco Negro" (and the tacit cries of Mãe Preta) to particular narratives and evocations of Japanese places and histories, the Mendes and Tsumori collaboration, adds another layer, turning the historical gaze (and ear) in part to the complexity of historical encounter of the Portuguese (and Jesuits) in Japan.[16]

Japan has produced a number of professional fado singers and instrumentalists over the past few decades; fado is a musical world that has been notoriously difficult for outsiders to enter (as musicians). Fado's circuits in Japan were shaped by the longstanding circulation of Amália's recordings there, including a Japanese release of her 1957 Olympia album in the 1960s, and her public performances.[17] The most celebrated was a 1970 Tokyo concert made into a live album, which as Vítor Pavão dos Santos notes, contains a "vertiginous Barco Negro" (2005 [1987], 274).

# September 2, 1970 Tokyo, Sankei Hall

Amália introduces "Barco Negro" in English. "Sorry. I wish I could speak Japanese. But I think the only thing I can say is *arigato* [and] *konbanwa* [good evening], nothing more." "I think that it is thanks to this song I have an international career. I made a film, a French film, and because it was French, everybody could see it. And I became an international singer . . .'Barco Negro,' it's a love song." (applause) . . . "We [Portuguese] came from people who helped to discover the world we live in today. I am going to sing a very sad song of Portugal, 'Black Boat.'"

Listen. There is the silk in her timbre. The tempo is faster than in her 1957 Olympia album, the instrumentalists virtuosic, and her voice one of ease, invention, and absolute control. There is her anticipation and driving of the beat with her vocal entrances. There are her moves from pianissimos to the arcs in which her voice swells in volume on the "são loucas" and the ways in which she sustains the long notes with tremendous breath. Listen to the playfulness, born of mastery, in her ornamentations, even while crying in song. Listen to her voice in the height of its power.[18]

# **8** Fados About Fado: "Tudo Isto É Fado" and "Que Deus Me Perdoe"

For listeners who understand the words, self-reflexive fado lyrics can play a role in teaching something about fado protagonists, places, its fadistas and instrumentalists, and its stereotypical emotions, sometimes linking feeling to sound, instruments, or voice. I call these self-reflexive fado poems "meta-fados" (or fados about fado). Meta-fados help to shape a biographical and historical narrative of the genre, sometimes personifying it. This commentary is sometimes repetitive and uses variations on stock phrases (for example, like *guitarras a chorar* [crying guitarras], *uma voz dolorida* [a painful voice]) and stereotypical to the genre. While a number of the lyrics on the Olympia album comment on fado in some way, "Tudo Isto É Fado" (All of this is fado) and "Que Deus Me Perdoe" (May God Forgive Me [for loving fado]) both stand out for the way their lyrics reflexively comment on a fado genre world of feeling. When Amália sings meta-fados about fado feelings, fado's emotional power is partially defined through her vocal timbre. With the ebbs and flows of the intensity of her voice (with her shifts in volume, the force of her breath, her speeding or slowing of the tempo, and with her shifts in timbre) she dwells in a highly charged emotional register and then pulls away, circles back, hovers, and returns. In these fados about fado feeling Amália's voice becomes the wrenching sound that signals those feelings.

# "Tudo Isto É Fado" (All of This is Fado)

Track 5: side A

"C'est ça le fado"
If you want to become my master, and to have me forever, don't talk to me only about love, talk to me also about fado. Since you don't know what it is, I will tell you.

*translation of excerpt from French lyrics*
*summary from back jacket*

"Tudo Isto É Fado" (lyrics by Anibal Nazaré, music by Fernando de Carvalho) was first written for a musical theater (or *revista*) show and was later adopted by Amália; Rodrigues omits the first half of the lyrics in the version she sings on this album (Santos 2014, 232). If she had sung these lines (as she does in most other recorded versions), you would have heard lyrics that set up the story as a teaching moment, "You asked me the other day / If I knew what fado was / I said that I didn't know / ... But I will tell you now." Even without the first lines, it is clear that the song is a meta-fado. Amália begins with the second half of the fado, with lyrics that address a male suitor, saying that if he wants to be hers then he better not just talk to her about love, but that he must also talk to her about fado. The lyrics continue, marking fado as a "punishment" (*castigo*), fado as "everything that I am saying, and that which I don't know how to say." They mark fado as a language, or alternate reality, with meanings beyond what words can convey. The lyrics of the refrain gesture toward this elusive meaning in the form of a list, giving fado a place (the ancient Lisbon neighborhood of Mouraria, one of fado's originary places), a protagonist (a ruffian [*rufia*] who sings), instruments that possess voice and feeling (guitarras that cry), emotions (love, jealousy, pain). And here fado is also "defeated souls," "lost nights," "bizarre shadows," and "pecado" (sin) and "cinzas e lume" (ashes and flame). The final words of the refrain bring it all together (All of this exists / All of this is sad / All of this is fado).

# "Que Deus Me Perdoe" (May God Forgive Me [for loving fado])

Track 5: side B

> "Que Dieu me pardonne"
> May God forgive what I do, if it is a crime or a sin. I sing because I cannot say [in words] all that I suffer in the depths of my soul.
>
> > *translation of excerpt from French lyrics*
> > *summary from back jacket*

Listen carefully to the very beginning of this track. An instrumentalist strums a tone almost simultaneously with the audience applause. As Amália begins to announce the title of the fado, the guitarrista plays a brief lick which brings instrumentalists, Amália, and the listeners into the sound world and the musical key of the fado before starting.

This fado-canção (lyrics by Silva Tavares, music by Frederico Valério) is a meta-fado that showcases the relationship between the protagonist of the song, (the "I"), and her "inner self," to the act of singing fado. On the one hand, in this poem, singing fado is capable of purging the fadista of thoughts of all that is bad in life, and through singing "dreaming an immense dream" (*sonhar sonho imenso*) that everything is happiness." On the other hand, singing fado here is capable of giving voice to a soul that is "closed" (*alma fechada*), a soul that cries in song (*choro a cantar*), and to make audible the hidden and silent parts of the self ("by singing I am heard / and nothing hurts me" [*cantando dou brado / e nada me doí*]). These lyrics also (as in "Tudo Isto É Fado") link fado to sin, the singer asks God to forgive her for singing the fado "if it is a crime or a sin" (*se é crime ou pecado*). This casting fado as "sin" recalls fado's origin stories connected to brothels, to "vice," and perhaps gestures implicitly to fado's first female celebrity fado figure, the nineteenth-century fado singer and prostitute Maria Severa, who, as legend has it, brought fado from its bohemian margins to the upper classes through her romantic liaison with a count.

There are so many breathtaking moments in Amália's performance of this fado on this recording in terms of her vocal ornamentation, her expressive use of vibrato, dynamics, play with meter, and the way in which she divides phrases in relation to her breathing. The first comes at her entrance, with her styling of the word "alma" (soul) with a descending four-note ornament. Another comes on the phrase "e a sonhar sonho imenso" (and to dream an immense dream) (2:16). The instrumentalists stop playing as she prolongs, and draws attention to the word "sonhar" (to dream) with a descending *voltinha*, that last note of which floats in the air before a last-minute ascent. She finishes the phrase with the two words "sonho imenso," just in the nick of time and the instrumentalists catch her. Adding heightened drama, on the final phrase of the fado, she takes a breath and drops her volume on the words "Que Deus me" (that God) (3:54), prolonging them and trailing off to almost a whisper on the word "me" before inhaling again and then releasing the breath on the final word "perdoe" (forgive). It swells with sound. Frenetic rapid strums of the guitarrista. Applause. More applause. Amália, "Merci … obrigada …merci bien."

# Interlude II: Mid-Century Representations: Simone de Beauvoir's *Les Mandarins*

The French philosopher and writer, Simone de Beauvoir published her novel *Les Mandarins* in 1954; it won the French literary prize, the Prix Goncourt, in the same year. It was published in English translation in 1956. Early in *The Mandarins*, two of the novel's central characters, Henri and Nadine, travel to Lisbon. Henri remarks on the beauty of the city, "its quiet heart, its unruly hills, its houses with pastel-colored icing, its huge white ships" (Beauvoir 1991 [1956], 94). They are taken by the contrast between postwar Paris, and its scarcity, and the sumptuous bounty they find in Lisbon's luxury shops (Scholz and Mussett 2005, 6). There they find: leather gloves, "poplin shirts," beautiful leather shoes "that you could walk in without getting your feet wet," silk and wool, rich hot chocolate "overflowing with whipped cream" (Beauvoir 1991 [1956], 95).

To some extent, the novel reflects Beauvoir's own experience and challenges in thinking through multiple political contradictions in the post-World War II moment (Scholz and Mussett 2005, 4–7).[1] In her portrayal of Henri's and Nadine's experience in Lisbon, Beauvoir is also attuned to internal contradictions within Lisbon itself, and between Portugal's outward-facing representations and the lived realities of the vast majority of its people.

Venturing into a working-class neighborhood in the historic center (likely the neighborhood of Mouraria adjacent to Graça), Henri describes what he witnesses:

> Barefooted women—everyone here went barefooted— were squatting before their doors frying sardines over charcoal fires, and the stench of stale fish mingled in the air with the smell of hot oil. In cellar apartments opening onto the street, not a bed, not a piece of furniture, not a picture; nothing but straw mats, children covered with rashes, and from time to time a goat. Outside, no happy voices, no laughter, only somber, dead eyes. Was misery more hopeless here than in other cities? Or instead of becoming hardened to misfortune, does one grow more sensitive to it? The blue of the sky seemed cruel above the unhealthy shadows ...
>
> Beauvoir 1991 [1956], 96

The following day, Henri attends a party at the French Consulate; a former Portuguese cabinet minister remarks to him, "all that writing about the melancholy of the Portuguese and how mysterious it is. Actually, it's ridiculously simple: of seven million Portuguese, there are only seventy thousand who have enough to eat" (Beauvoir 1991 [1956], 97). He gives Henri a tour of Lisbon the next morning, intended to show him some of what is behind the "beautiful façade" of the city, hoping that the French may learn "the truth"; he wants Henri to see first-hand, "what the people eat, how they live" (Beauvoir 1991 [1956], 97). He brings Henri to visit "a series of wretched hovels" (Beauvoir 1991 [1956], 97). Later in the day, he introduces Henri to his friends:

> They were mostly former cabinet members, former journalists, former professors who had been crushed because of their obstinate refusal to rally to the new regime. They were poor and trapped, many had relatives in France who had been deported.... They wanted to believe that the destruction of Nazism would somehow bring to an end this hypocritical fascism, and they dreamed constantly of overthrowing Salazar and creating a National Front like the one which had been formed in France. But they knew they were alone: the English capitalists had large interests in Portugal and the Americans were negotiating with the government for the purchase of air bases in the Azores. "France is our only hope," they repeated over and over. "Tell the people of France the truth," they begged. "They do not know; if they knew they would come to our rescue."
>
> Beauvoir 1991 [1956], 97–78

Simone de Beauvoir's *Les Mandarins*, the film *Les Amants du Tage,* NATO's "Introducing Portugal" short film, and the album *Amalia à l'Olympia* all offer representations of Portugal and Lisbon at midcentury intended primarily for a foreign (non-Portuguese) public. There are overlaps and frictions, resonances and dissonances between them.

# **9** Diva Constellations

Divas and their voices might be understood by their publics as extraordinary. The voice of a particular diva might be experienced as singular in the intimacy through which it moves us. Yet, at the same time, to be a diva or a vocal celebrity is to belong to the genre of the diva, a genre of celebrity.[1] How might we understand the place of this album (and the making of Amália's celebrity) in relation to politics and networks of audibility, histories of commercial sound recording and consumption, and the shaping of the mid-twentieth century international vocal celebrity?

*Amalia à l'Olympia* (1957) is situated in between two pivotal moments in relation to the history of Anglo and European music recording industries. In the first, in the early decades of the twentieth century, representatives from big record companies in places like Britain and Germany traveled to peripheral port cities in Europe and Northern Africa to record vernacular urban genres and voices. These companies produced these recordings on 78 rpm shellac discs and exported them back to their communities of origin (Denning 2015, 78). Michael Denning (2015) has written about this moment, between the mid-1920s and early 1930s, in terms of an "audiopolitics of a world musical revolution." In the second, in the 1980s–1990s, a new strategy for marketing recorded music from outside Anglo and European economic centers emerged. Advances in digital recording technology vastly facilitated the extraction, sampling, and recontextualization of recorded sound. Scholars Steven Feld, Louise Meintjes, and Timothy Taylor have written about that moment in relation to "schizophonic-mimesis" (Feld 1996), "world beat" and "world music" (Meintjes 1990), "global pop" (Taylor 1997), and the "politics of amplification" (Feld 1993).

The moment in the middle, the one in which Amália Rodrigues' 1957 Olympia album is situated, is marked by the beginning of the golden age of the 33 1/3 rpm "Long Play" record along with the florescence of new forms of media and intermediality, or relations between different forms of media (for example, between sound recordings, television, radio, and film). The emergence of commercial international air travel facilitated both elite forms of tourism and the travel of musical celebrities on concert tours. Increasingly, multiple nations promoted tourism as an economic and political strategy, promoting nationalism and international visibility.

As Denning notes, that earlier twentieth century moment of the recording and circulation of vernacular musics shifted the focus to the "idiosyncrasies of vocal timbre," marking a change from the song being the most important to the singer being the most valued by the music industry (2015, 183). By midcentury many of the "vernacular" forms that Denning writes about are consolidated as national, and music tourism begins to take off (2015, 225–227), including early fado tourism in Portugal. Bruno Coquatrix, in his strategy for the revival of the Olympia Music Hall, even factored Parisian tourism into his business equation, especially for its summer season, and the success of the hall as an "international prestige spot" depended on programming "top international names."[2] During this time the genre of the "travel" or "holiday" LP emerges (Borgerson and Schroeder 2017; Elliot 2014). In midcentury, both the recording and the tourism industries play roles in solidifying links between musical genres and representations of the nation, partially setting the stage for the "world music" phenomenon of the 1980s and 1990s, and priming relationships between music, "heritage," and tourism that thrive in many parts of the world today.

It is not only these relationships between musical genre and nation that are being consolidated in midcentury. *Vocal celebrity itself is consolidated and codified as a genre of its own.* In this moment, and for some decades to follow, the Olympia Music Hall, under Bruno Coquatrix, serves as a key venue (in a key city) through which international vocal celebrity is amplified and the international prestige of his venue and the international prestige of his stars are interdependently shaped. Within this context, international vocal celebrities were sometimes shaped in relation to one another, while at the same time being specifically framed in terms of the nation, and sometimes serving, implicitly or explicitly, as musical cultural ambassadors.

In the case of Amália, her celebrity, vis-à-vis the stage and platform of the Olympia, was initially strategically framed and made legible to Parisian audiences partially in relation to Édith Piaf's (see Chapter 1). Piaf's recurring presence on the Olympia stage had been fundamental to the hall's revival under Bruno Coquatrix; in 1960–1961, a series of her performances there saved the hall from bankruptcy (Looseley 2015, 9). Amália Rodrigues, in interviews with her in Santos' book, often refers to her proximity to other celebrities at the time (including Piaf, whom she talks about as someone whom she greatly admired, but also as a friend) demonstrating that she travels in their orbit (Gray 2013, 193; Santos 2005 [1987], 123). Her claim that, "in France they called me the Portuguese Piaf, in Arab countries I was the Oum Kalthoum and in Mexico it was Chelo Flores" (Santos 2005 [1987], 101), points to the ways in which mid-twentieth-century vocal celebrity was in part shaped through shared frameworks of legibility.

Musical celebrities would sometimes pass works in their repertoires between one another, often altering them in the process, and giving them heightened international circulation and audibility; examples include Dalida's transformation of "Barco Negro" (with Caco Velho's music) into "Madona" (see Chapter 7) and and Louis Armstrong's and Bing Crosby's separate adaptations of "Coimbra" ("April in Portugal") (which Amália sang on the Olympia album).[3] Then there are the audiovisual gatherings of vocal celebrities in the 1950s, as in the Mexican color film, *Música de Siempre* (1958) (starring, among many others, Édith Piaf, Amália Rodrigues, and the Peruvian singer Yma Sumac).[4]

In relation to repertoire choice on the Olympia album, to some extent, Amália's voice, as extracted from her live 1956 concerts, was made to sound more "Portuguese" than in the live performances (for example, not including a song she performed in Spanish). David Looseley, in his cultural history of Édith Piaf, notes something similar in relation to Piaf's performances in New York, where she represents an essentialized American ideal of France (2015, 115). While Piaf was becoming the sound of the French for New York audiences, Rodrigues was being shaped as the voice of Portugal. Looseley writes about how Piaf's image postwar, as the "voice of France," is an image "refracted through an American lens," a representation that is then exported back to France. In making this argument he draws on the work of Richard Kuisel, who writes about the ways in which France, during the postwar period, is shaped from the perspective of the United States, as America's "other" (Kuisel 1993, 6 as cited in Looseley 2015, 114). Piaf's representation as a French national icon is, to some extent then, "refracted" from the mirror that is the music and culture industry in the postwar U.S. (Looseley 2015, 115). For Amália Rodrigues, as the "voice of Portugal," the most powerful refractions are cast from a three-way mirror, triangulated between Portugal, France, and the United States and the key cities of Lisbon, Paris, and New York (and Hollywood). At the same time, Amália's Olympia album launched in a moment marked by "the fastest growth in popular music ever seen in France" (Lebrun 2013, 90). Portugal, in terms of geography, economic resources, and international visibility and power, was on the periphery, and the conduit of France helped to amplify Amália's celebrity and voice for an international and European public.

A driving political force for this moment, concerns the reconfiguring of strategic alliances in the postwar period, against a backdrop of increasing political precariousness of European colonial projects. Within this context, the nation itself becomes a product for export and music, musicians, and their recordings key players in exporting representations of the nation, some musicians intentionally or unintentionally serving as ambassadors of the nation (Fiol-Matta 2017; Von Eschen 2006). These representations of the nation for export, in a moment of such a radical political reconfiguration of alliances, can be fraught with ambivalence or occlusions. Licia Fiol-Matta, in her book, *The Great Woman Singer*, reminds us that the voice is always "covered by gender" (2017, 5).[5] She explains how vocal celebrities during this time often labored under the "pressure to perform values," under the weight of transmitting symbolism and ideologies of the nation, including values about gender (2017, 3, 5). In so doing, they exported versions of femininity itself as a genre (Berlant 2008).

Amália Rodrigues was no exception. The pain and pathos many of the song lyrics on the Olympia album reference, channeled so powerfully through Amália's voice, are mostly about nostalgia, rosy depictions of Portuguese places, or heterosexual romantic love, these sentiments partially serving as a haze that occludes the realities of poverty, inequity, or of dictatorship, or of colonialism. At the same time, this album is also a powerful testament to Rodrigues' artistry, her creative musicality, her savvy programming for an international public, to the affective force of her voice, her drama, and her presence. It is all these things while, at the same time, also serving as a vehicle for a certain presentation of Portugal (and of femininity, female vocality, and of romantic love).

For much of her career, Rodrigues was caught in a political cross-fire, building and sustaining a career during Portugal's dictatorial regime, and serving as a musical ambassador for Portugal, even while some in her closest circle were on the political left. She claimed publicly to be apolitical, even on the occasion when she sang a love song "Abandono," that made coded references to political prisoners (Santos 2005 [1987], 139 as cited in Gray 2013, 190). Following the revolution in April 1974, fado fell out of favor with some on the political left, due to its perceived role as a propaganda tool of the dictatorship. Some fado houses closed during this time. For Amália Rodrigues, this post-revolution moment was particularly difficult, in that some of her public in Portugal turned against her, accusing her of being complicit with the regime.

After her death in 1999, the Portuguese author and Nobel laureate José Saramago, announced that Amália had been clandestinely giving money to the communist party during the regime (the communist party played a key role in orchestrating the revolution).[6] This ambivalence, reflected in relationships between her public biography, her politics, and her private affairs continue to be a subject of polemic and interest in Portugal today.[7] Amália consistently walked a fine line on politics, her political ambiguity in her public presentation of self, perhaps a strategy for her enduring power (Gray 2013, 189–194). Today, some younger Portuguese musicians, such as the queer activist fado group Fado Bicha (Silva 2018) and the musical ensemble Deolinda (Gray 2016) draw on fado's divergent histories as both social critique and as a censored form that helped maintain the status quo during the regime, overtly shaping alternate public musical–political narratives from fados' ambivalent past to change the tenor of politics of the present.

## *resonances: A Portuguese House* "Uma Casa Portuguesa"

In the summer of 2018, I see graffiti scrawled in red cursive letters on a high white wall in Lisbon's Alfama neighborhood which reads, "'A Casa portuguesa foi arrendada pelos turistas,' Amália Rodrigues" (The Portuguese home was rented to the tourists, [signed by] Amália Rodrigues). To the right of the red graffiti, a scribbled dialogue has unfolded on the wall in blue and neon green, in English, French, and Portuguese. "#Fuck AirBnb," "*Cassez vous*" [Go away!], "~~NON~~" (no), "SIM" (yes).

This graffiti refers to the song "Uma Casa Portuguesa" (see Chapter 5) implicitly invoking its symbolism as stereotypical Portuguese home and hearth. The author of the words playfully signs the critique with Amália's name, even though the words are not hers, and belong to the contemporary moment. By signing Amália's name and bringing "Uma Casa Portuguesa" into the present, the author of the graffiti in red invokes Amália's voice and persona as the "soul" of Portugal, and a key song in her repertoire, but in ironic commentary. By 2018, partially in response to the 2011 financial crisis in Portugal, state-sanctioned projects of foreign housing investment, in tandem with a rapid escalation in tourism, facilitated by low-cost airline travel and short-term rental companies like Airbnb, had created a dire crisis in affordable housing. By 2018, the fado neighborhood of Alfama had few remaining local residents and almost no essential businesses left (Gray 2018).[8] But new venues in Alfama claiming to offer authentic fado seemed to be increasing by the day, along with souvenir shops selling Lisbon memorabilia made in China. In the fado museum at Alfama's base, right across from the river Tagus, where massive cruise ship cities park in a gleaming new port, a permanent exhibit on the career of Amália Rodrigues repeats (on a loop) the clip of her singing "Barco Negro," from the film *Les Amants du Tage*, the film that she claimed garnered her that invitation from Bruno Coquatrix to sing at the Olympia Music Hall in Paris in 1956.

Lisbon's tourism tsunami in the second decade of the twenty-first century, and fado tourism today, do not directly derive from Amália's international success. But that mid-1950s moment, in terms of international travel, nationally promoted tourism, the age of the LP, the marketing of travel albums, can be understood as a prehistory of the music tourism of today. The version of Lisbon, fado, and Portugal that is currently sold to tourists, has something in common with the rosy and saudade-filled depictions of place found in *Les Amants du Tage* or on Amália's first Olympia album.

Amália Rodrigues' 1957 Olympia album is so many things at once. It could be understood as a souvenir token of sorts, not only for those who may have attended "live," but also for those who have never been to Paris, nor to Portugal, who might acquire a bit of the aura of liveness, of "being there," of the cosmopolitanism of Paris and of the Olympia, or a feeling of the place they imagine as Portugal (a kind of virtual sonic tourism), through their experience with, and ownership of, the album as sung through the voice of Amália. The album is a tangible record of Rodrigues' debut on the Olympia stage, a mark of having arrived, when to "arrive" in Paris was to arrive to a certain idea of belonging to the world (to a listening public that *mattered*.) This object (the album) circulates, its circulation lending her more prestige and increased celebrity while at the same time bringing increased prestige for the Olympia.

On the back of the album, above the endorsement by the Portuguese poet and cultural attaché in Paris, Luís Chaves de Oliveira (see Chapter 4), is a large logo of the Olympia Music Hall, a bright yellow circle streaked with orange ("*l'Olympia: votre music-hall*") with the underlined signature of Bruno Coquatrix beneath it in black. Bruno Coquatrix's Olympia is the resonating chamber for Amália's voice, amplifying it, and the 33 1/3 "live" album bringing this voice, and an experience of Coquatrix' newly revived postwar Parisian music hall, to applauding listeners, a listening public that Oliveira situates as vast, as coming from the "four corners of the earth."

While her repeated Parisian successes and the Olympia album greatly amplified her voice and celebrity and helped to define the genre of fado outside of Portugal, the story of internationalism that this album tells is not just about Paris (nor just principally about Lisbon, Paris, and New York). This album is a container for stories, that spin out in divergent and sometimes overlapping directions and that touch down in so many places, and is shot through with so many different kinds of networks, musical and political histories, sound worlds, and geographies. There is Portugal's peripheral geopolitical status as a dictatorship on the far westernmost corner of Europe, and its emergence into postwar NATO positioning and Atlanticist diplomacy. There are circuits of music and culture industry between New York, Paris, and Hollywood. There are the networks and proximities between Lisbon and Madrid, Portugal and Spain, and Amália's prior marketing in the United States as an "Iberian" artist who sang fado and flamenco. Then there are the well-worn colonial circuits and histories, reflected in the social histories of some of the songs on the album (like "Uma Casa Portuguesa" and "Barco Negro"), between Portugal and Angola, or Portugal and Mozambique, or Lisbon and Rio de Janeiro.

# Coda: "Fado Amália"

Track 7 (final track): side B

"Amália"
    God wanted me to be called Amália; it's a very popular name and I can't help but find it amusing when I hear "Amália sing me a fado!"

*translation of excerpt of French lyrics*
*summary on the back jacket*

The fado song "Fado Amália" (lyrics by José Galhardo and music by Frederico Valério) is in the lyric style of meta-fado. Rather than commenting on the genre of fado itself, the lyrics of "Fado Amália" reflexively comment on a character named "Amália." As with many of the lyrics on this album, the song narrative is saturated with an idea of romantic love. Here the character of "Amália" sometimes blurs with Amália Rodrigues the fadista, the celebrity. Amália, in performing this fado, inhabits both the first person, "I" and comments on "Amália" in the third person. In the first verse, "Amália" is amused when she hears someone scream "Amália, sing me a fado." And in the second verse, it is the character of "Amália" who cries while singing ("Amália chora a cantar") because "until one dies, to love is to suffer." The strategic position of this meta-fado as the final track on the album works to cement a celebrity phenomenon of "Amália" where "Amália," and her voice, that "cries in song" is larger than her one life, existing outside of herself, a subject for reflection in song. Listen to how she starts by ornamenting the name "Amália," with descending *voltinhas*, with her voice as she sings it for the first time. Listen to how she styles the name differently each time it comes around. Listen until the very end where thunderous clapping and shouts from the audience fill the music hall of the Olympia. Applause.

# Notes

## Notes on the Text

**1** Rodrigues, Amália. 1957. *Amalia à l'Olympia*. France: Columbia FSX 123, 33 1/3 rpm.

## Preface: A Yearning for Liveness

**1** In the title of the original French album, and in many materials written in languages other than Portuguese, "Amália" is spelled without the accent on the second letter A. I include the accent in her name in the title of this book out of respect for the Portuguese but maintain the spelling of her name as it appears in the original source materials (for example, in French or English language critic reviews or album titles) in subsequent usages.

## 1 Dresses, Acrobats, and the Sound of Moonlight

**1** Santos, Maria Manuela Gomes dos. 2018. Personal communication with author, June 29.

**2** Amália Rodrigues is often simply known by first name, as "Amália." I use "Amália," "Amália Rodrigues," and "Rodrigues" interchangeably.

**3** "L'Olympia, Paris." 1954. *Variety,* June 16, 1954, 55.

**4** *O Jornal.* 1956. Rio de Janeiro. April 14, 1956, 6 and *O Globo.* 1956. Rio de Janeiro, May 29, 1956, Matutina Geral, 5 (as cited in

Santiago 2020, 40, 42). "Los Cascabeles" likely refers to "Doce Cascabeles" (music by R. Freire, lyrics by Cabello and Solano), which Amália also recorded for this album: Rodrigues, Amália. 1954. *Amalia Rodrigues Sings Fado from Portugal [and] Flamenco from Spain*. New York: Angel Records ANG-64002, 33 1/3 rpm.

**5**  Santiago, Frederico. Interview with the author. Lisbon, Portugal. June 25, 2018. Mp3 format.

**6**  See Daphne Brooks on her read of Jackie Kay's work on Bessie Smith's trunk (in Kay's 1997 biography of blues icon Bessie Smith): "In Kay's hands, the storied Bessie Smith's trunk amounts to an archive of the incomplete. . . . Kay takes stock of the objects that carry the residue of the departed blues woman's sensorial life" (2021, 312, 313).

**7**  *Programme de Gala de Music-Hall*. 1956. Paris: l'Olympia, April 30, 1956.

**8**  Pitet, Jean-François. 2012. "May 1958: Cab Calloway at the Olympia in Paris." *The Hi de Ho Blog.* September 13. Available at: www.thehidehoblog.com/blog/2012/09/may-1958-cab-calloway-at-the-olympia-in-paris.

**9**  Paris, Nogrady. 2021. "Les Akeff, jeux icariens," (undated photographs). Centre national des arts du cirque, fonds Ariane, Touzé. BnF, Éditions multimédias. Available at: https://cirque-cnac.bnf.fr/fr/search/node/les%20akeff.

**10** "Darvas and Julia 1949: Rehearsal VIII." 1949. Archivio Cameraphoto Epoche by Carlo Pescatori. Photograph. Accessed March 3, 2021. Available at: www.starsinvenice.com/darvas-and-julia-1949/2736-56936-rehearsal-i.html.

**11** Brokate, Geoff. 2018. "Revolution in Paris." *Open Skies,* January 24, 2018, 57–61. Available at: https://www.emirates.com/co/english/open-skies/4749989/revolution-in-paris.

**12** Willsher, Kim. 2018. "Marilyn Stafford's best photograph: Albert Einstein in his lounge," *The Guardian,* January 3, 2018. Available at: www.theguardian.com/artanddesign/2018/jan/03/marilyn-stafford-best-photograph-albert-einstein.

**13** Willsher, Kim. 2017. "How a chance meeting with Einstein led to the accidental start of a unique photography career." *Los Angeles Times*, December 4, 2017. Available at: https://www.latimes.com/world/europe/la-fg-britain-stafford-photographer-20171204-story.html.

**14** Dany, Marcel. 1956. "Entre um número de saltimbancos e outro de acrobatas, Amália Rodrigues delicia os parisienses que consideram o fado uma canção com luar." *O Século*, April 23, 1956, 1, 2.

**15** Santos, Maria Manuela Gomes dos. 2022. Personal communication with author, July 1.

# 2  Biographies of Her Voice

**1**  For more extended discussion on her afterlife in Portugal, see Gray 2013, 179–235.

**2**  See Carvalho 2020 and Carminho 2020.

**3**  Franco, Acácio. 2021. "Gravações de Amália Rodrigues candidatas a 'Memória do Mundo' da UNESCO." *Observador*, October 6, 2021. Available at: https://observador.pt/2021/10/06/gravacoes-de-amalia-rodrigues-candidatas-a-memoria-do-mundo-da-unesco/.

**4**  See Gray 2013, 188–189, Domingos 2020, 887–888, and Nery 2020, 8–9 on the power of Santos' text (and some of the limitations of this text) in shaping Amália's public biography.

**5** Basic biographical and chronological details in this section are culled from Gray 2013, Nery 2010 and Santos 2005 [1987]. For a source in English on the biography of Amália Rodrigues, see; Almeida, Bruno de, director. 1999. *The Art of Amália*. Written by Bruno de Almeida, Frank Coelho, and Vítor Pavão dos Santos. Arco Films. 35mm. 90 minutes.

**6** Disc records of 78 rotations per minute (rpm), emerged in the late 1800s and were superseded by 33 1/3 rpm vinyl discs in 1948. For basic discussion of the history of recording formats see: British Library Learning: n.d. "From Phonautographs to Mp3s." Accessed October 23, 2022: Available at: www.bl.uk/history-of-recorded-sound/articles/timeline-of-formats.

**7** Kemp, Robert. 1949. "Découverte du fado." *Les Nouvelles Littéraires*, Paris, April 14, 1949 (cited in Santiago [2020, 30]).

**8** Rodrigues, Amália. 1954. *Amalia Rodrigues Sings Fado from Portugal [and] Flamenco from Spain*. New York: Angel Records ANG-64002, 33 1/3 rpm.

**9** "New Angel Blue Label Popular Recordings for May: Introducing a New Personality: Amalia Rodrigues in Fado and Flamenco Songs." 1954. *News from Angel Records*. Bulletin No. 11, May 6, 1954.

**10** "Fado is fascinating, fado is the fad." 1954. Angel Records advertisement. *The Billboard*. May 29, 1954, 58.

**11** Verneuil, Henri, dir. 1955. *Les Amants du Tage*. France: TF1 International-Gaumont. (Les Films du Collectionneur). 110 min. 2008. DVD. (See Santos 1987 [2005], 245 for a list of cinemas and premiers in Paris, Lisbon, and London.)

**12** See for example, Rodrigues, Amália. 1955. *Amalia of Portugal*. New York: Angel Records ANG 64013, 33 1/3 rpm.

**13** See Looseley 2015, 28, 115 with respect to Édith Piaf.

**14** Rodrigues, Amália. 1958. *Amalia Rodrigues Chante en Français*. Ducretet-Thomson 460 V 391, EP.

**15** *Correio da Manhã*. 1956. Rio de Janeiro. June 10, 1956, 6 (as cited in Santiago, 2020, 42).

# 3  A *Fado* Primer

**1**  I write here about the genre of Lisbon fado (*fado de Lisboa*). Lisbon fado is a distinct genre from the genre of fado associated with the university city of Coimbra (although in practice there is some overlap). For more on histories, forms, and practices of Lisbon fado, in English, see: Brito 1994, Colvin 2016, Elliott 2010, Gray 2013; Nery 2012; Vernon 1998. See Gray 2007 and 2013 for more extended discussion on the themes in this chapter.

**2**  For example, see Holton 2016 on fado YouTube generation performers in the United States.

**3**  See Gonçalves 2022 on fado practice, the generational transmission of learning, and the micro-dynamics of community making in contemporary Lisbon.

**4**  For more extended discussion of fado form and improvisation, see Castelo-Branco 1994, Carvalho 1999, Gouveia 2010 and Gray 2013, chapter 4.

**5**  "Fado: Portuguese soul music." 2019. Hosted by Rajan Datar with guests: Simon Broughton, Lila Ellen Gray, and Rui Vieira Nery. BBC *The Forum*. Produced by Fiona Clampin. Podcast, MP3 Audio, 41 minutes, May 4. Available at: www.bbc.co.uk/programmes/w3csyp4m.

**6**  An example of a female singer using "pianinhos" can be heard in a 2003 recording of the fadista Argentina Santos singing the fado "As Minhas Horas" (My hours) at 3:30–3:35 (Santos, Argentina. 2003. *Argentina Santos.* Companhia Nacional de Música CMN100CD, compact disc).

**7** An example Amália using a descending glissando can be heard on the word *olhos* (eyes) in the track "Barco Negro" on her 1957 Olympia album (:44–:45).

**8** "Amália Rodrigues no Tribunal da Opinão Pública," 1965. *Riso e Ritmo.* RTP 1. RTP Arquivos, television program. Available at: https://arquivos.rtp.pt/conteudos/amalia-rodrigues-no-tribunal-da-opiniao-publica/.

**9** Rodrigues, Amália. 1970. *Com Que Voz.* Columbia SPMX 5012, 33 1/3 rpm.

See Gray 2013, chapter 6 for more extended discussion of themes in this section.

# 4 Listening to Amália

**1** Rodrigues, Amália. 2005. *Amália Rodrigues: Live in New York (1990).* IMM Music Ltd. IMM 940073, DVD and compact disc.

**2** The title of the fado poem that she sings on this album (set to the traditional fado form of *fado corrido*) is "Lá Porque Tens Cinco Pedras," by Linhares Barbosa. Neither the original disc nor the album jacket state the name of the poem.

**3** Rodrigues, Amália. 1976. *Amalia à l'Olympia: Les Succès d'Amalia Rodrigues.* Japan: EMI/Odeon EOS-70091, 331/3 rpm.

**4** Rodrigues, Amália. 1970. *Amalia Rodrigues in Japan at Tokio Sankei Hall, 2nd September 1970.* Japan: EMI-Odeon OP-80084, 331/3 rpm.

**5** *O Jornal.* 1956. Rio de Janeiro, May 20, 1956, 6 (translated from the Paris *L'Express*) (as cited in Santiago 2020, 22).

**6** See Santiago 2020, 21–23.

**7** See Hinton 1980 as discussed in Ninoshvili 2009, 419.

**8** See Gray 2013, chapter 5, and Cook 2003 for additional aspects of gender or "the woman" as represented in fado.

# Interlude I: Mid-Century Representations: "Introducing Portugal"

**1** "Portugal and Nato." n.d. *North Atlantic Treaty Organization*. Accessed January 19, 2022. Available at: www.nato.int/cps/en/natohq/declassified_162352.htm?utm_source=ytdesc&utm_medium=smc&utm_campaign=190509%2Bportugal.

**2** "Introducing Portugal." 1955. *The Atlantic Community Series*. North Atlantic Treaty Organization. Film. 17:58. Accessed January 15, 2022. Available at: www.nato.int/cps/en/natohq/declassified_162352.htm?utm_source=ytdesc&utm_medium=smc&utm_campaign=190509%2Bportugal.

**3** "Marcha do Centenário" (March of the Centenarian) (music by Raúl Ferrão, lyrics by Norberto de Araújo).

# Prelude: On Love and Longing

**1** *Programme de Gala de Music-Hall*. 1956. Paris: l'Olympia, April 30.

# 5 Presentation and "Uma Casa Portuguesa" (A Portuguese House)

1 Fonseca, Artur, Vasco [de] Matos Sequeira, and Reinaldo Ferreira. 1953. *Uma Casa Portuguesa*. Lisbon: Valentim de Carvalho. BNL Deposito Legal 200217 23.11153. (Note: the cover of the score erroneously lists "Artur Ferreira" as the composer of the music.)

2 See Pacheco, Nuno. 2007. "Casa portuguesa." *Público.* March 28, 2007. Available at: www.publico.pt/2007/03/28/jornal/casa-portuguesa-181784. See also Matos 2008, 111 and Santos 2014, 493 for more on the history of this song.

3 See Hess, Peter. 2014. "Eusébio, A Life in the Shadows of the Colonial Past." *Culture Contexts: Essays on Global Issues, Present and Past*. Blog. January 5, 2014. Available at: https://sites.utexas.edu/culturescontexts/tag/lourenco-marques/.

4 Digitized versions of these recordings are archived online at the Instituto Moreira Salles. Available at: https://discografiabrasileira.com.br/fonograma/name:in/casa portuguesa.

5 Pacheco, Nuno. 2017. "Uma casa portuguesa, sem certezas nenhumas." *Público.* September 21, 2017. Available at: www.publico.pt/2017/09/21/culturaipsilon/opiniao/uma-casa-portuguesa-sem-certezas-nenhumas-1785942.

6 Mísia. 2015. *Para Amália*. Warner Music 2564602198, compact disc.

7 Pacheco, Nuno. 2017. "Em defesa de Mísia, de Amália e do fado." *Público.* September 14, 2017. Available at: www.publico.pt/2017/09/14/culturaipsilon/opiniao/em-defesa-de-misia-de-amalia-e-do-fado-1785284.

# 6 "Perseguição" (Pursuit)

1 Rodrigues, Amália. 1995. *Pela Primeira Vez: Rio de Janeiro 1945*. EMI Valentim de Carvalho 8348672, compact disc.

2 Alice, Maria. 1936. "Perseguição." Poem by Avelino de Sousa and music by Carlos da Maia. *Minha Mãe/Perseguição*. Columbia DL 98, 78 rpm.

3 Zambujo, António. 2010. "Apelo." Poem by Vinícius de Moraes and music by Carlos da Maia. *Guia*. France: World Village WVF479049, compact disc.

4 A digitized version of her 1936 recording is archived at Lisbon's fado museum. Available at: https://arquivosonoro. museudofado.pt/repertorios?search=Perseguicao. (I am indebted to the fadista António Rocha for teaching me about performance nuances of this fado in my lessons with him in 2002–2003.)

5 See also Nery 2009, 165.

6 Abreu, Ester de. 1952. "Perseguição." Poem by Avelino de Sousa and music by Carlos da Maia. *Perseguição/Reflete Amor*. Sinter 00-00165, 78 rpm.

A digitized version is archived at the Instituto Moreira Salles. Available at: https://discografiabrasileira.com.br/.

# 7 "Barco Negro" (Black boat)

1 See also Nery 2009, 166 for a discussion of Amália's "são loucas" in this recording.

2 Conjunto Tocantins. 1943. "Mãe Preta." Caco Velho and Piratini. Continental 15107, 78 rpm.

A digitized version is archived at the Instituto Moreira Salles. Available at: https://discografiabrasileira.com.br/fonograma/name/mae preta.

3 See also Lopes and Nogueira 2019, 4 and Oliva 2016, 79 on the "batuque" designation in "Mãe Preta" and Silva 2019, 216 on the performative vestiges of the *batucada*, in Amália's renditions of "Barco Negro"; all three articles offer perspectives on socio-musical histories (and afterlives) of "Barco Negro."

4 Conceição, Maria da. 1954. "Mãe Preta," Caco Velho and Piratini. Odeon 13691. The recording is available online at the Instituto Moreira Salles at https://discografiabrasileira.com.br/fonograma/name/mae preta.

5 See, for example, listings on the used recording marketplace/database site Discogs. n.d. Accessed October 17, 2022. Available at: www.discogs.com/release/12231181-Maria-Da-Concei%C3%A7%C3%A3o-M%C3%A3e-Preta-Disse-me-Disse-me-Disse-me.

6 See also Saganfredo 2020 quoting Arthur de Faria on the "irony" that the samba ("Mãe Preta") was "transformed into a fado with music composed by a black Brazilian sung by a Portuguese singer."

7 Seganfredo, Thaís. 2020. "Trajetória de Caco Velho, o 'sambista Infernal' de Porto Alegre." *Jornal do Comércio*, November 11, sec. Reportagem Cultural. Available at: https://www.jornaldocomercio.com/_conteudo/especiais/reportagem_cultural/2020/11/766392-trajetoria-de-caco-velho-o-sambista-infernal-de-porto-alegre.html.

8 Dalida. 1956. "Madona" on *Dalida Chante*. By Caco Velho, Piratini, and M. Lanjean. Barclay 70034, 45 rpm.

**9** See also Lebrun (2013, 89–90; 2020, 41–43) for discussion of Dalida's repertoire choice in the mid-1950s, and the song "Madona," in relation to evoking a Mediterranean exoticism where the Mediterranean is rendered "geographically elastic and timeless" (2020, 41).

**10** See Seganfredo 2020 for discussion of Caco Velho and intellectual ownership/rights regarding Melachrino's version of "Barco Negro." Melachrino, George, conductor. 1958. The Melachrino Orchestra. *Lisbon at Twilight*. RCA SF-5034, 33 1/3 rpm.

**11** Mariza. 2001. *Fado em Mim*. Times Square Records New York and World Connection, Haarlem, the Netherlands WC 43028, compact disc.

**12** Mariza. 2021. *Mariza Sings Amália*. Nonsuch B08NWQZT3L, compact disc.

**13** Lina and Raül Refree. 2020. *Lina_Raül Refree*. Glitterbeat GBLP085, 33 1/3 LP.

**14** Rosalía. 2017. *Los Ángeles*. Produced by Raül Refree. Spain: Universal 0602557392296, LP.

**15** Mendes, Miguel Gonçalves. 2021. *O Sentido da Vida*. Paris Filmes. Film. 120 min.

**16** See also: Mendes, Miguel Gonçalves and Giovane de Sena Brisotto. 2015. "Barco Negro: O Fado Japonês de Kumico Tsumori." *Expresso*, October 8. Available at: https://expresso.pt/blogues/o-sentido-da-vida/2015-10-08-Barco-Negro---o-fado-japones-de-Kumico-Tsumori.

**17** Rodrigues, Amália. 1965. *Amalia à L'Olympia*. Odeon OR 7117. Japan. Mono 33 1/3 rpm.

**18** Rodrigues, Amália. 1970. *Amalia Rodrigues in Japan at Tokio Sankei Hall, 2nd September 1970*. OP-80084. EMI-Odeon, 33 1/3 rpm.

# Interlude II: Mid-Century Representations: Simone de Beauvoir's *Les Mandarins*

1   Scholz and Mussett frame their edited volume of philosophical essays on *The Mandarins* around the "various contradictions of freedom" (2005, 1) that Beauvoir treats in her novel.

# 9 Diva Constellations

1   See Koestenbaum 1993 and Roach 2007.

2   "L'Olympia, Paris." 1954. *Variety*, June 16, 1954, 55.

3   See Elliott 2014, for discussion of "Coimbra"/"April in Portugal" iterations within the context of "holiday records" and nostalgia.

4   Davison, Tito, director. 1958. *Música de Siempre*. Allianza Cinematografica Mexicana. Film.1h20m.

5   Here Fiol-Matta notes that she is "riffing on Hortense Spillers (2003, 378), who spoke of a subject 'covered by race.'"

6   Pedro, Ana Navarro. 1999. "José Saramago em Paris: 'Amália fez chegar dinheiro ao PC,'" *Público*, October 9, 1999, 9.

7   See Carvalho 2020.

8   See also Sánchez-Fuarros 2016, on fado tourism and urban renewal; and Santos 2019 on tourism gentrification and housing in contemporary Portugal.

# References

Ávila, Elaine. 2021. *Fado: The Saddest Music in the World*. Vancouver, B.C.: Talonbooks.

Baptista, Tiago. 2009. *Ver Amália: Os Filmes de Amália Rodrigues*. Lisbon: Tinta-da-China.

Beauvoir, Simone de. 1991 (1956). *The Mandarins*. Translated by Leonard M. Friedman. New York, N.Y.: W.W. Norton.

Béhague, Gerard. 2001. "Brazil." In *Grove Music Online*. Oxford University Press. Available at: https://doi.org/10.1093/gmo/9781561592630.article.03894.

Berlant, Lauren. 2008. *The Female Complaint: The Unfinished Business of Sentimentality in American Culture*. Durham, N.C.: Duke University Press.

Borgerson, Janet, and Jonathan E. Schroeder. 2017. *Designed for Hi-Fi Living: The Vinyl LP in Midcentury America*. Cambridge, MA.: The MIT Press.

Brito, Joaquim Pais de, ed. 1994. *Fado: Voices and Shadows*. Lisbon: Electa.

Brooks, Daphne A. 2021. *Liner Notes for the Revolution: The Intellectual Life of Black Feminist Sound*. Cambridge, MA.: Harvard University Press. Available at: https://doi.org/10.2307/j.ctv1dhph54.

Caille, Bernadette. 2009. "Amália Francesa." In *Amália: Coração Independente*, edited by Clara T. Vilar and Nuno Ferreira de Carvalho. Lisbon: Museu Colecção Berardo.

Carminho. 2020. *Amália, Já Sei Quem És*. Lisbon: Nuvem de Letras.

Carvalho, Miguel. 2020. *Amália: Ditadura e Revolução*. Alfragide, Portugal: Publicações Dom Quixote.

Carvalho, Ruben de. 1999. *Um Século de Fado*. Lisbon: Ediclube.

Castelo-Branco, Salwa El-Shawan. 1994. "The Dialogue Between Voices and Guitars in Fado Performance Practice." In *Fado: Voices and Shadows*, edited by Joaquim Pais de Brito, 125–141. Lisbon: Electa.

Colvin, Michael. 2016. *Fado and the Urban Poor in Portuguese Cinema of the 1930s and 1940s*. Rochester N.Y.: Tamesis.

Cook, Manuela. 2003. "The Woman in Portuguese Fado-Singing." *International Journal of Iberian Studies* 16(1): 19–32. Available at: https://doi.org/10.1386/ijis.16.1.19/0.

Costa, António Firmino da and Maria das Dores Guerreiro. 1984. *O Trágico e o Contraste: O Fado no Bairro de Alfama*. Lisbon: Publicações Dom Quixote.

Danielson, Virginia. 1997. *The Voice of Egypt: Umm Kulthum, Arabic Song, and Egyptian Society in the Twentieth Century*. Chicago IL.: University of Chicago Press.

Denning, Michael. 2015. *Noise Uprising: The Audiopolitics of a World Musical Revolution*. London: Verso.

Domingos, Nuno. 2020. "Amália Rodrigues e o Século XX Português." *Análise Social* 55 (237): 886–897. Available at: https://doi.org/10.31447/AS00032573.2020237.09.

Elliott, Richard. 2010. *Fado and the Place of Longing Loss, Memory and the City*. Ashford: Ashgate.

———. 2014. "'Time and Distance Are No Object.'" *Volume !. La Revue des Musiques Populaires* 11(1) (December): 131–143. Available at: https://doi.org/10.4000/volume.4204.

Feld, Steven. 1993. "The Politics of Amplification: Notes on 'Endangered Music' and Musical Equity." *Folklife Center News* 15(1): 12–15.

———. 1996. "Pygmy POP. A Genealogy of Schizophonic Mimesis." *Yearbook for Traditional Music* 28: 1–35. Available at: https://doi.org/10.2307/767805.

Fiol-Matta, Licia. 2017. *The Great Woman Singer: Gender and Voice in Puerto Rican Music.* Durham N.C.: Duke University Press.

Fox, Aaron A. 2004. *Real Country: Music and Language in Working-Class Culture*. Durham N.C.: Duke University Press.

Gil, José. 2007. *Portugal, Hoje: O Medo de Existir*. Lisbon: Relógio D'Água.

Gonçalves, Ana. 2022. "Local Event, Family and Music: The Rootedness of Cultural Heritage." In *Family Events: Practices, Displays and Intimacies*, edited by Thomas Fletcher, 87–99. London and New York: Routledge.

Gouveia, Daniel. 2010. *Ao Fado Tudo Se Canta*. Linda-a-Velha: DG Edições.

Gray, Lila Ellen. 2007. "Memories of Empire, Mythologies of the Soul: Fado Performance and the Shaping of Saudade." *Ethnomusicology* 51(1): 106–130.

———. 2011. "Fado's City." *Anthropology and Humanism* 36 (2): 141–163.

———. 2013. *Fado Resounding: Affective Politics and Urban Life.* Durham N.C.: Duke University Press.

———. 2016. "Registering Protest: Voice, Precarity, and Return in Crisis Portugal." *History and Anthropology* 27(1): 60–73. Available at: https://doi.org/10.1080/02757206.2015.1113409.

———. 2018. "Listening Low-Cost: Ethnography, the City, and the Tourist Ear." In *The Routledge Companion to the Study of Local Musicking*, edited by Suzel Reily and Katherine Brucher, 2017–28. New York, N.Y.: Routledge.

Hinton, Leanne. 1980. "Vocables in Havasupai Song." In *Southwestern Indian Ritual Drama*, edited by Charlotte Frisbie, 275–305. Albuquerque N.M.: University of New Mexico Press.

Holton, Kimberly DaCosta. 2016. "Fado in Diaspora: Online Internships and Self Display among YouTube Generation Performers in the U.S." *Luso-Brazilian Review* 53(1): 210–232.

Kay, Jackie. 1997. *Bessie Smith*. Bath: Absolute Press.

Koestenbaum, Wayne. 1993. *The Queen's Throat: Opera, Homosexuality, and the Mystery of Desire*. New York, N.Y.: Poseidon Press.

Kuisel, Richard F. 1993. *Seducing the French: The Dilemma of Americanization*. Berkeley CA.: University of California Press.

Lebrun, Barbara. 2013. "Daughter of the Mediterranean, Docile European: Dalida in the 1950s." *Journal of European Popular Culture*. 4(1): 85–97.

———. 2020. *Dalida: Mythe et Mémoire*. Marseille: Let Mot et le Reste.

Lino, Raul. 1998 [1944]. *Casas Portuguesas*. Lisboa: Cotovia.

Looseley, David. 2015. *Édith Piaf: A Cultural History*. Liverpool: Liverpool University Press.

Lopes, Guilhermina, and Lenita W. M. Nogueira. 2019. "Mãe Preta: Releituras e Ressignificações de Uma Canção Brasileira." *Música e Cultura* 11(1): 36–58.

Matos, Maria Izilda Santos de. 2008. "Âncora de Emoções: A Imigração Portuguesa." *Cadernos CERU* 19(1): 99–113. Available at: https://www.revistas.usp.br/ceru/article/view/11846/13623.

Meintjes, Louise. 1990. "Paul Simon's Graceland, South Africa, and the Mediation of Musical Meaning." *Ethnomusicology* 34(1): 37–73. Available at: https://doi.org/10.2307/852356.

Meizel, Katherine. 2011. "A Powerful Voice: Investigating Vocality and Identity." *Voice and Speech Review* 7(1): 267–74. Available at: https://doi.org/10.1080/23268263.2011.10739551.

Melo, Daniel. 2001. *Salazarismo e Cultura Popular (1933–1958)*. Lisboa, Portugal: Imprensa de Ciências Sociais.

Munslow, Barry. 2005. "Maputo." In *Encyclopedia of African History*, edited by Kevin Shillington. New York: Fitzroy Dearborn. Available at: credoreference.com.

Nery, Rui Vieira. 2004. *Para uma História do Fado*. Lisbon: Corda Seca, Público.

———. 2009. *Pensar Amália*. Lisbon: Tugaland.

———. 2010. "Rodrigues, Amália de Piedade Rebordão." In *Enciclopédia da Música em Portugal no Século XX*, edited by Salwa Castelo-Branco, P-Z:1132–38. Lisbon: Temas e Debates/ Círculo de Leitores.

———. 2012. *A History of Portuguese Fado*. Translated by David Cranmer. Lisbon: Imprensa Nacional-Casa da Moeda.

———. 2020. "Prefácio: Amália e Manuel da Fonseca: Entre a Cumplicidade e o Jogo do Gato e do Rato." In *Amália nas Suas Palavras: Entrevista Inédita a Manuel da Fonseca Em 1973*, transcribed by Pedro Castanheira 7–19. Porto: Porto Editora.

Ninoshvili, Lauren. 2009. "The Poetics of Pop Polyphony: Translating Georgian Song for the World." *Popular Music and Society* 32(3): 407–424.

Oliva, Osmar Pereira. 2016. "Travessias do 'Barco Negro': O Sequestro da Mãe Negra." *Interdisciplinar – Revista de Estudos em Língua e Literatura* 25 (May–August): 77–94. Available at: https://seer.ufs.br/index.php/interdisciplinar/article/ view/5749.

Pereira, Paulo Manta. 2020. "'Urbanistic Architecture' According to Raul Lino: Visions of the Portuguese City in the First Half of the Twentieth Century (1900–1948)." *Enquiry The ARCC Journal for Architectural Research* 17(1): 1–27. Available at: https://doi.org/10.17831/enq:arcc.v17i1.1064.

Roach, Joseph. 2007. *It*. Ann Arbor, MI.: University of Michigan Press.

Rollo, Maria. 2011. "1945–1959 The Post-War Period and the Beginning of the European Venture." *CVCE*. Available at: www.cvce.eu/obj/1945_1959_the_post_war_period_and_the_beginning_of_t he_european_venture-en-1ef6d8a2-e7a0-47c3-bfdd-a7f3d499c9fe.html.

Sánchez-Fuarros, Iñigo. 2016. "'Ai, Mouraria!' Music, Tourism, and Urban Renewal in a Historic Lisbon Neighbourhood." *MUSICultures* 43 (2): 66–88. Available at: https://journals.lib.unb.ca/index.php/MC/article/view/25475/29519.

Santiago, Frederico. 2020. "Amália em Paris: Do Olympia Parti para o Mundo." Liner Notes. In *Amália em Paris*. Portugal: Edições Valentim de Carvalho, compact disc.

Santos, Ana Cordeiro. 2019. *A Nova Questão da Habitação em Portugal: Uma Abordagem de Economia Política*. Coimbra: Actual.

Santos, Vítor Pavão dos. 2005 (1987). *Amália: Uma Biografia*. Lisbon: Editorial Presença.

———. 2014. *O Fado da Tua Voz: Amália e os Poetas*. Lisboa: Bertrand.

Silva, Daniel da. 2018. "Unbearable Fadistas: António Variações and Fado as Queer Praxis." *Journal of Lusophone Studies* 3(1): 124–147. Available at: https://doi.org/10.21471/jls.v3i1.213.

———. 2019. "Black Mothers and Black Boats: Queer, Indigenous, and Afro-Brazilian Intersections in Ney Matogrosso's 'Mãe Preta (Barco Negro).'" *Journal of Lusophone Studies* 4(1): 208–227. Available at: https://doi.org/10.21471/jls.v4i1.305.

Scholz, Sally J., and Shannon M. Mussett. 2005. "Introduction." In *The Contradictions of Freedom: Philosophical Essays on Simone de Beauvoir's* The Mandarins, edited by Sally J. Scholz and Shannon M. Mussett, 1–32. Albany N.Y.: State University of New York Press.

Spillers, Hortense J. 2003. "All the Things You Could Be by Now, If Sigmund Freud's Wife Was Your Mother: Psychoanalysis and

Race." In *Black, White, and in Color: Essays on American Literature and Culture*, 376–427. Chicago, IL.: University of Chicago Press.

Taylor, Timothy D. 1997. *Global Pop: World Music, World Markets*. New York/London: Routledge.

Tinhorão, José Ramos. 1994. *Fado: Dança do Brasil, Cantar de Lisboa*. Lisbon: Caminho da Música.

Urban, Greg. 1991. *A Discourse-Centered Approach to Culture: Native South American Myths and Rituals*. Austin TX: University of Texas Press.

Vernon, Paul. 1998. *A History of the Portuguese Fado*. Aldershot: Ashgate.

Von Eschen, Penny M. 2006. *Satchmo Blows up the World: Jazz Ambassadors Play the Cold War*. Cambridge MA.: Harvard University Press.

Yano, Christine Reiko. 2002. *Tears of Longing: Nostalgia and the Nation in Japanese Popular Song*. Cambridge MA.: Harvard University Press.

# Index